ENGLISH LIFE IN THE MIDDLE AGES

OXFORD UNIVERSITY PRESS
AMEN HOUSE, E.C. 4
London Edinburgh Glasgow New York
Toronto Melbourne Capetown Bombay
Calcutta Madras
HUMPHREY MILFORD
PUBLISHER TO THE UNIVERSITY

FIRST PUBLISHED 1926
REPRINTED 1927, 1928, 1937, 1941

May Festivities: c. 1500

The party in the boat are going for a picnic, with their wine-flask hanging
over the side.   In the market square men are dancing.

ENGLISH LIFE IN THE MIDDLE AGES

By

L. F. SALZMAN, M.A., F.S.A.

Author of 'Medieval Byways'
'English Industries of the
Middle Ages', &c.

OXFORD UNIVERSITY PRESS
LONDON: HUMPHREY MILFORD

TO NANCY

PREFACE

THE objects of a text-book should be first to stimulate interest, secondly to satisfy that interest up to a certain point, and thirdly to indicate to those who wish to travel beyond that point by what paths they may attain to fuller knowledge. The two first of these objects I have endeavoured to keep before me while writing this book, and the third is partially fulfilled by my Bibliography.

Bearing in mind the fact that the book is intended for schools and for students who are not already experts in the matters treated of, I have confined myself to the more important or characteristic features of each subject, and have striven to state them as simply and lucidly as possible. For the same reason, when I have quoted medieval English writers I have not hesitated to modernize the spelling or even to substitute a modern word for its obsolete equivalent when I considered that the original would be a stumbling-block in the way of the unwary. My quotations are important for their meaning, and it is more essential that the reader should grasp that meaning than that he should have the exact original before his eyes and be left to gape amazedly at unfamiliar combinations of vowels and consonants. But no one will be more pleased than myself if any readers are moved to turn to those originals and tackle them for themselves. The Social Life of the Middle Ages can only be properly understood by the intimate study of the vast mass of confused and fragmentary remains which that life has left behind, and it is from no foolish modesty that I would point to the illustrations, taken from medieval sources, as in some ways the most valuable part of the whole book.

CONTENTS

The World of Good and Evil

The inhabitants of the Heavenly City look out over the City of Human Life, which is divided into seven sections, each representing one of the Seven Deadly Sins and the corresponding Virtue. In the centre Sloth and Industry ; to the right Avarice (gambling) and Generosity ; above this Gluttony and Temperance, Lechery and Chastity ; to the left of the centre Anger and Patience ; above this Envy and Courtesy, Pride and Humility.

LIST OF ILLUSTRATIONS

I

INTRODUCTION

RUDYARD KIPLING, writing about private soldiers in the days before the Great War, when they were not popular with the general public, protested that they were not ' plaster saints ' but human flesh and blood, ' most remarkably like you '. There is a general tendency to think of medieval men and women as if they were such saints or devils as we see on churches, carved in stone ; but the more we study them the more we realize that they were flesh and blood, most remarkably like us. Edward I, ' the Greatest of the Plantagenets ' and ' the Hammer of the Scots ', is a fine figure of a king, but he takes on a new interest for us when we find him buying toys—a gaily painted crossbow or a model cart—for his children and paying forfeits to the ladies of the court if they can catch him in bed on Easter Monday morning, or when we read his letters to his mother and find him making the same sort of feeble little intimate jokes that we make in our letters home. Human nature was very much the same in the Middle Ages as it is now ; few of us are at our brightest and best before breakfast, and it is pleasant to find a writer in the twelfth century saying of one of the Norman conquerors of Ireland : ' This man was such that in the morning he was peevish and irritable, but after eating generous and good-tempered, courteous and liberal to all.'

But if human nature was much the same, the conditions of life were very different, and if we are to understand our ancestors we must try and look at the facts of their lives from their own points of view. Our standards of living, of comfort, and morality, are very different from those of the Middle Ages, by which term we mean the thousand years from the conquest of Britain by the Saxons to the reign of Henry VIII, and more particularly the last five hundred years of that period. Even during those five hundred years standards changed very much in some ways, but, taking the period as a whole, the Middle Ages are fairly sharply separated from modern times by the changes which took place in the sixteenth century. If we wish to realize the conditions of medieval life by looking at existing conditions we must turn not to modern England but to such a district as the Balkan States, where life is lived—or was, up to the time of the late war—in very much the same way as it was in England in the fourteenth century.

Because the modern and medieval standards of living are different, it does not follow that either is ' higher ' or ' lower ' than the other. That the homes of the greatest Norman barons lacked the ' bath (h. and c.) and usual offices ' found in the humblest houses of to-day does not alter the fact that those lords lived in luxury : they had every comfort that they could imagine, and therefore they were just as luxurious as any modern millionaire surrounded by every comfort that *he* can think of ; for luxury, and even comfort, is entirely a matter of comparison. We need not waste our pity upon our ancestors ; they did not require it. Life is always the same in all periods ; namely, comfortable for the rich and less comfortable for the poor, their sense of discomfort being determined by the luxury which they feel they might have and cannot get ; so that we may say that the most comfortable state of society is that in which there is least difference between the poor and the rich ; and such

A May Day Riding Party: c. 1416.

a state was to be found in the early Middle Ages rather than in the present age. Moreover, comfort is not the same thing as happiness ; and if we have discovered a great deal about the art of making ourselves comfortable, we have lost something of the art of getting joy out of life. This is natural, for in the Middle Ages the nation was in its youth, and joy is the mark of youth as comfort is of the elderly ; for example, the young can enjoy the simple pleasures, and even the simple discomforts, of camping out, while their elders prefer to sit down in dull comfort to punctual meals where the food is unromantically free from the flavour of wood smoke, and to sleep in beds which are neither upraised by mole-hills nor frequented by earwigs. The closer we look at medieval England, the more we shall feel inclined to picture it as young and hardy and joyous. To begin with, the country was full of colour. The churches glowed with stained glass and painted walls ; the dresses of the wealthy, men as well as women, were gorgeous and brilliant, and if the peasantry wore more serviceable russets and browns and blues, they usually managed to introduce a splash of red or other bright colour in their hoods or kerchiefs. And the country was full of song. Though the English were not so devoted to music as the Welsh or the Irish, and though the men of the south country were, even in the twelfth century, less tuneful than the northerners, yet they were a musical race ; and with the singing went dancing, and nowhere did the country dance flourish more than in England. FitzStephen, who wrote a description of London at the end of the twelfth century, tells of the dancing in the fields, which brought to a close a holiday full of the excitement of horse-racing, games of ball and mimic tournaments. His whole account of a holiday crowd in, or rather outside, London is full of the joy of life, and may be compared with a modern bank-holiday crowd on Hampstead Heath by any one who thinks that the people of Norman England were dull barbarians :

' Every year on Shrove Tuesday the schoolboys delight themselves all the forenoon in cock-fighting ; after dinner all the youths go into the fields to play at ball. The scholars of every school have their ball or staff in their hands ; the ancient and wealthy men of the city come forth on horseback to see the sport of the young men and to take part in the pleasure of beholding their agility. Every Friday in Lent a company of young men comes into the field on horseback, and the best horseman conducteth the rest. Then march forth the citizens' sons and other young men, with blunt lances and shields, and there they practise feats of war. In the Easter holidays they fight battles on the water. A shield is hanged upon a pole fixed in the middle of the river ; a boat is prepared, to be carried down by the swift stream, without oars ; in the fore part thereof standeth a young man ready to give charge upon the shield with his lance ; if so be he breaketh his lance upon the shield and doth not fall, he is thought to have performed a worthy deed. If so be without breaking his lance he runneth strongly against the shield, down he falleth into the water, for the boat is carried swiftly with the tide ; but on each side of the shield ride two boats, with young men, which rescue him that falleth as soon as they may. Upon the bridge, wharfes and houses by the riverside stand great numbers to see and laugh thereat. In the holy days all the summer the youths are exercised in leaping, dancing, shooting, wrestling, casting the stone, and practising their shields ; the maidens trip to their timbrels and dance as long as they can well see.'

Some four hundred years later John Stowe records how he had ' in the summer season seen some upon the river of Thames rowed in wherries, with staves in their hands, flat at the fore end, running against one another and, for the most part, one or both overthrown and well ducked '. But the Middle Ages were giving place to a more staid and sober age when Stowe was an old man, and he regretfully records that ' the youths of this City have also used on holy dayes after Evening prayer, at their maisters' doors, to exercise their cudgels and bucklers ; and the maidens, one of them playing on a timbrell, in sight of their maisters and dames, to daunce for garlandes hanged athwart the streetes ; which open pastimes of my youth being now suppressed, worser practises within doores are to be feared '.

Yet we must not ignore the dark side of medieval life. Disease was rampant. The cities and country towns were as destitute of any regular system of sanitation as they still are in Turkey or the Balkans. From time to time plague and pestilence swept through the country, and the terrible Black Death, which carried off a third of the population and in some places left not sufficient survivors to bury the dead, was only the worst of many outbreaks.

Skin diseases were rife, owing to the lack of personal cleanliness, and every town had its leper hospitals outside its walls and its lepers wandering through its streets, seeking alms from the charitable and clacking continuously their wooden clappers to warn the citizens from coming into contact with them. The death-rate amongst young children must have been appalling ; Henry III and Edward I each had at least five children who died in infancy, and even if the families of the poor, who could not afford to feed their infants on unwholesome luxuries or to employ doctors with their well-meant but disastrous medicines, had a better chance of survival, it is certain that in all classes of society the proportion of children that died young was very large. Of those that reached manhood many, owing to bad food and other causes, were diseased or crippled. The towns were full of these unfortunates, unable to work and compelled to beg their living. But if they had no workhouse infirmary to which they could go and no modern system of relief and doles to support them, yet the lot of the poorest was in some ways less hard than it is now. They could retain their self-respect ; poverty was looked upon as an affliction but not as a crime, and all men in the Middle Ages would have been shocked at the idea of imprisoning a cripple or feeble old man for begging or for being ' without visible means of subsistence '. Able-bodied beggars might incur the wrath of the Law and the Church for their idleness, ' for no one is in a state of salvation who does no profit to the world '—as Archbishop Peckham declared when he excommunicated the lazy Welshmen—but the Acts of Mercy, which should be performed by all true Christians, included the feeding of the poor and the clothing of the naked, and the giving of alms was one of the chief duties set forth by the Church. Even a man so little given to good works as King John was lavish in this one respect ; on Good Friday in 1203 we find him paying the equivalent of £80 in modern money for the feeding of a thousand poor persons, and during the month of May in the following year he caused a farthing loaf and a dish of gruel to be given daily to three hundred paupers in London and to another eighteen hundred in other parts of the

A Leper: c. 1500

*He carries in his hand a wooden clapper, to warn
passers-by that he is unclean*

*Charity, a Queen, inspired by her Guardian Angel
to give alms to a Beggar: 14th century*

kingdom.   Similarly, Edward I paid for the food of 666 poor persons every Sunday and fed seventeen hundred poor on the occasion of his son's seventeenth birthday.

These figures are some evidence of the number of persons who were so poor as to need charity for their comfort if not for the absolute maintenance of life.   For them the writer of *Piers Plowman* pleads :

> The neediest are our neighbours if we give heed to them,
> Prisoners in the dungeon, the poor in the cottage,
> Charged with a crew of children and with a landlord's rent.
> What they win by their spinning to make their porridge with,
> Milk and meal, to satisfy the babes,
> The babes that continually cry for food—
> This they must spend on the rent of their houses ;
> Aye, and themselves suffer with hunger,
> With woe in winter, rising a-nights
> In the narrow room to rock the cradle.
> Pitiful is it to read the cottage women's woe,
> Aye and many another that puts a good face on it,
> Ashamed to beg, ashamed to let neighbours know
> All that they need, noontide and evening.
> Many the children, and nought but a man's hands
> To clothe and feed them ; and few pennies come in,
> And many mouths to eat the pennies up.
> Bread and thin ale are for them a banquet,
> Cold flesh and cold fish are like roast venison ;
> A farthing's worth of mussels, a farthing's worth of cockles,
> Were a feast for them on Friday or fast-days ;
> It were charity to help these that be at heavy charges,
> To comfort the cottager, the crooked and the blind.

Besides the blind, lame, and maimed whose misfortunes were due to accident or disease, there were numbers of mutilated men whose injuries had been inflicted by the Law.   Medieval law, especially after the Norman Conquest, was savage and vindictive, and the criminal who escaped hanging was liable to have a foot or a hand struck off or to be blinded and mutilated in other ways. It was a period when life was held cheap and cruelty was almost a matter of course.   The clergy harped incessantly upon the eternal torments of Hell which awaited impartially the most abandoned ruffians, women who painted their faces, and men who failed to pay their tithes ; the lawyers hanged and mutilated men for the theft of a few shillings ; the Church and the Law joined hands to burn heretics ; and when Church and Law lost control of affairs, as in the Anarchy of Stephen's reign, the lawless wrought such horrors that ' men said openly that Christ and his saints were asleep '. Even in their sports there was often a note of cruelty, as in the favourite amusement of baiting bulls and bears, or in the schoolboys' sport of throwing at cocks, to say nothing of the less obvious cruelty involved in the training of the performing bears and other animals that were so popular in the Middle Ages.

Yet all this disease and poverty and cruelty could not quench the note of joy, and the Middle Ages were full of laughter. Humour played a very large part in medieval life. Often the humour was of the kind that appeals to the childish and un-developed mind—the practical joke and the indecent story. One mark of this childishness was the practice of nobles keeping in their households half-witted ' fools ' (as distinguished from the clever, irresponsible jesters), whose antics and unexpected sayings amused them. Preachers occasionally protested against this mockery of these ' innocents ', ' God's merry jesters ', whom the heathen Saracens treated with consideration as being specially under the protection of God, and one such preacher bluntly told his audience that if they found fools amusing they had better buy a looking-glass ; but the practice continued until the end of the medieval period. Popular humour, however, is to be seen in such things as the nicknames which the people bestowed upon one another. Until the thirteenth century the mass of the population had no true surnames, passing from father to son, but were known by their baptismal name, often with the name of their father added for distinction—just as at the present time in the Balkans half the males are known as George son of Demetrius and the other half as Demetrius son of George, which tends to confusion. To assist identification it became usual to add either the name of the place where the person lived, or his

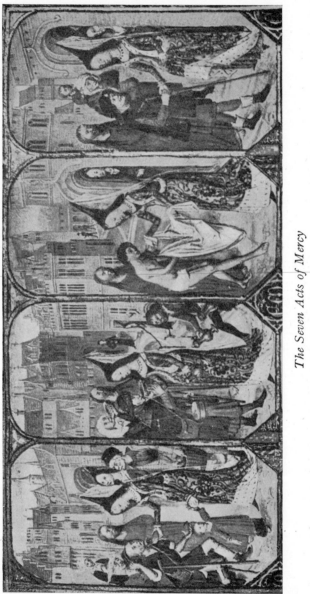

The Seven Acts of Mercy

(1) *Feeding the hungry* (2) *Giving drink to the thirsty* (3) *Clothing the naked* (4) *Hospitality*

The Seven Acts of Mercy

(5) *Visiting those in prison* (6) *Visiting the sick* (7) *Providing burial for the dead* (8) *Margaret, Duchess of Burgundy (sister of Edward IV), and her patron St. Margaret*

trade or something descriptive of the person himself. Often these descriptions were obvious physical traits, such as Long and Short, Brown and Russell (= red-haired) ; or fancied resemblance to some animal, such as Bull, for a powerful, thick-set man, or Litelmus (= little mouse) for his exact opposite ; but often there is something of the humorous quickness to notice little tricks of behaviour or speech which is still particularly noticeable among city urchins. So we find in the thirteenth century quantities of names, such as, William Stepsoft, William Barefoot (he was grandson of Philip Friday, as readers of *Robinson Crusoe* who remember the footprint in the sand might have expected), Mabel Yokedogge, John Wryngtayl, Patrick Pluckehenn, Alice Writhecol (who evidently was always twisting her neck about), Swetemilk (who probably called that commodity in the streets), and Souremilk (who very likely sold it as sweet), Gotobed, and even a Norman gentleman who had the strange and romantic name of Dieu-sauve-les-dames (God save the ladies !).

Humour is still more prominent in medieval art ; the margins of elaborately decorated books are full of grotesque figures and groups ; animals with human heads, knights mounted on snails tilting at one another, hares shooting at dogs, and monkeys playing all kinds of tricks. So too the carvings, in stone and wood, in our churches abound in humorous subjects—the amusing or satirical fancies of the workmen who carved them. Popular literature also is full of jokes, not always very refined and sometimes, as in burlesque imitations of the Bible or of the services of the Church, profane, according to modern ideas. In the Middle Ages, however, men did not hesitate to mingle laughter with their religion ; in the ' miracle plays ', which were designed to teach biblical history in a popular form, there was often a great deal of boisterous, knock-about humour, and even the stories with which preachers illustrated their sermons were often more amusing than edifying. But their religion was very real to our ancestors ; so real and closely associated with their lives, perhaps, that they did not see any reason to keep it separate from their humour. Even in their religion, however, there was much of the undeveloped child mind which we have seen was characteristic of the Middle Ages. On the one hand, there was a childlike simplicity and literalness of belief, which enabled them to accept the teaching of the Church without question ; on the other, a childish love, not unmixed with terror, of the strange, which led them to see miracles—of both good and evil spirits—in every unusual occurrence. One consequence of this is that medieval literature is full of stories of witchcraft and ghosts. Solemn historians will sandwich in between their accounts of battles and the deaths of kings some story of a man who stumbled upon the fairies at their revels and stole their golden cup, of a merman who was captured off the Essex coast, of a witch whose body was carried off by demons from the church wherein it lay, or of the ghost of a wicked priest who returned to haunt his parish and slew those who dared to face him.

So far we have been considering the mental characteristics of our ancestors and trying to indicate, very roughly and broadly, how they looked at life. But there are also certain points concerning the organization of society which must be dealt with. There has never been a period in historic times when all men have been equal, and in making general statements about the conditions of life at any period we have constantly to modify those statements so far as they concern a particular class of society. During the Middle Ages, at least after the Conquest, society may be divided first into two halves—the clergy and the laity. The clergy, whose concern was, in theory, with spiritual matters, looked to the Pope as their earthly head, had their own law and courts, and stood apart from the laity, whose head was the king. Further, we may divide the laity into three classes—nobles, traders, and labourers, which three classes we may see reproduced in the clergy by the prelates (the bishops and great abbots and priors), the ' regular ' clergy (monks and friars—the professional men of religion), and the ordinary parish priests and chaplains.

While these classes of society are distinct, the dividing lines between them are not very definite. Even the distinction between clergy and laity tended in practice to become obscure. The Conqueror's half-brother, Odo, was both Bishop of Bayeux and Earl of Kent; the Bishops of Durham were not only spiritual heads of their see but also lords of the Palatinate of Durham, and, therefore, on one side of their seals they are shown in episcopal vestments, and on the other mounted and clad in full armour. A writer in the twelfth century complains of the way in which the prelates would copy the nobles :

'Does the knight swear; then so does the bishop, and with far stranger oaths. Does the knight follow the chase; the bishop must go a-hunting. Does the one boast of his hawks; they are the other's only joy. Both ride abreast in the battle; and they sit side by side in the Court and the Exchequer, fellow-students who are become brother officers.'

At the other end of the scale was a crowd of lawyers, court officials, and clerks, who had received ' minor orders ', and were, therefore, entitled to the privileges of clergy, but at the same time were entirely employed in worldly affairs and were not debarred from marriage. So also, though the nobles and gentry formed a distinct landed and military aristocracy, there was no hard and fast line between them and the merchants or the yeomen : there was in England no such definite noble class as the *noblesse* of France, where all the sons and descendants of a noble inherited his nobility and were not allowed to soil it by trade or work. In England members of great families are constantly, and with increasing frequency, towards the end of the Middle Ages, found in the ranks of the traders or sinking to the level of the small farmers, while merchants rise to the position of gentry and even of peers of the realm. Even with the peasantry, although the greater number of them were unfree, bound down to the manor to which they belonged and practically the property of their lord, in actual practice they were very much better off than in theory. While they had no legal rights, beyond protection for their lives and limbs, against their lord, they were practically on a level with free men as regards all persons but their lord, and even his power over them was considerably limited by custom. Moreover, while the restrictions on their movements and the demands upon their time and labour were irksome, there was no great sense of indignity attached to their serfdom. The passion for theoretical freedom and love of liberty as a thing to be desired and fought for did not take hold of the minds of men until the Renaissance brought back the philosophy and ideals of ancient Greece and put an end to the childlike acquiescence in the existing state of affairs, which marked the Middle Ages.

Seal of Bishop Hatfield of Durham : c. 1350.

II

COUNTRY LIFE

MEDIEVAL society was built upon the basis of Land. In striking contrast to modern conditions, a landless man was, at the time of the Norman Conquest and for some centuries afterwards, a strange being, rarely to be found except in a few of the bigger towns. The vast majority of the population had a direct personal interest in agriculture and possessed a portion of land— it might be only a tiny patch of garden round a tumble-down hovel or it might amount to thousands of acres scattered throughout a score of counties ; it might be held by the service of acting as marshal of the king's army in time of war or by the humble service of acting as ploughman and carter to some local squire, but it was a portion of English soil to which the holder could point as definitely his own. And, on the whole, the owner of the garden patch was less likely to lose his land than the owner of broad estates, which the king might view with envious jealousy. Moreover, every bit of land had its lord and the ultimate lord of all the land was the king. If a sparrow swooped down upon a grain of corn, he might be stealing a potential ear of wheat which would have gone straight into the king's own barn, or, far more probably, robbing John Doe, the humble tenant of Sir Geoffrey de Say, who held his land of the Earl of Surrey, who held his estates of the king. In the latter case, if John Doe ran away or died without heirs, the bit of land on which the sparrow was trespassing would come into the hands of Sir Geoffrey, and should he be guilty of certain crimes for which his lands were forfeited it would come to the Earl of Surrey, and if that noble were caught plotting treason, it would pass with the rest of his estates into the hands of the king. Whether, in these circumstances, our noble lord the king would send his archers and crossbowmen to slay the thieving sparrow is not the point, which is to show that if almost every man had a bit of land, every bit of land had at least one owner and often several, one above the other, and always with the king at the top. How this affected life in the Middle Ages, and how it came about is worth considering.

The earliest inhabitants of our island had paid little attention to agriculture. They lived mainly by hunting, and wandered about the country, settling down for a time where game was plentiful and the conditions of life bearable. In such a place they would pitch the wigwam huts required to shelter their family group, surrounding the cluster of huts with an earthen bank, a stockade, or some such form of protection : and since man cannot conveniently live on meat alone, a portion of the surrounding soil would be broken up with primitive ploughs and corn sown, to be gathered when ripe, rubbed and pounded to flour by the painful labour of women, and by them converted into cakes which should assist the survival of the fittest. Each successive season that the same piece of ground was sown with similar seed the yield would be less, and when the soil, or the supply of game, had become exhausted, the village would be abandoned and the family group would seek a new site, or, if their numbers had become too large for comfort, several new sites. At this time, and at this time alone, might it be said that the land belonged to the people ; there were no private rights in land, because there were no private individuals to assert them ; life apart from a community—a tribe or a family group—was practically unthinkable, and would undoubtedly be short, even if exciting.

By the time that the Romans came to Britain life had become more localized and more complicated. The village settlements had become larger and the settlers had acquired more personal possessions ; it was not quite such a simple matter as it had been to flit, like swarming bees, to a new hive. Some of the settlers now kept cattle and pigs, and not only did these (especially the pigs) add to the difficulties of travelling to a new site, but they played a large part in the rise of ideas of property and conflicting rights to the land. The man who had live stock had a source of wealth as well as of food, he had something to barter, that is to say to trade with ; but he had also acquired fresh responsibilities towards his neighbours. His cattle might graze at will over the unenclosed country, but if they strayed into the village corn there would be trouble, and if they ate up all the best grass down by the river so that other men's cattle had to fare scantily there would again be trouble, unless he had the support of his position as a chief or a priest. So there would be a tendency gradually to enclose the cornfield and the best meadows, to restrict the number of cattle that any one man might put into these meadows, and to reserve parts of the best grazing lands for the private use of the chiefs and great men. Moreover, with a larger population and more efficient ploughs, drawn by oxen, there would be a tendency for the lazier members of the settlement to shirk their duty of cultivating the common land. This was avoided by dividing up the cornfield into a large number of narrow strips and assigning several of these strips to each household, who were responsible for their proper cultivation. At first, no doubt the entire crop from the field continued to be the common property of the whole village, but, as responsibility and privilege always go together, the strips gradually came to be regarded as the property of the actual cultivators, and the corn from each strip would be taken by the household to whom the strip had been assigned.

When the Romans, a practical race with a considerable know-ledge of agriculture, conquered Britain, they introduced their own system. This system was based upon the ' villa ', or big country house and farm, with fields round it cultivated by slave

Agriculture : 15th century
Ploughing, sowing, harrowing, reaping, and binding sheaves

The Apple-harvest

labour. These fields were now the private property of the farmer, and the surplus crops, that is to say all that he did not require for the support of his household, would be sold—usually in the towns that were growing up under the Roman government. This system of farms, however, was only introduced in the central and southern portions of Britain and even in those districts large tracts were unaffected by it, so that when the Saxon invaders arrived, about the end of the fifth century, they

Building a Stockade round a Village.

must have found most of the land still being cultivated in big fields, divided into strips, as already explained. Under the Saxons an important change was made. Instead of growing crops year after year on the same big field until the soil was exhausted and then breaking up another piece of ground, the whole of the arable, that is the ground suitable for ploughing, was divided into two parts, which were cultivated in alternate years, so that half the land was always lying fallow, resting and recovering its goodness, while the other was under cultivation. By a later development the arable was divided into three parts, of which one lay fallow each year ; the fallow field being sown next year with wheat and the following year with oats or barley or peas and beans and then reverting to fallow again. These two schemes, known as the two-field and three-field systems, continued in use over the greater part of England all through the Middle Ages.

The Saxons came as an invading and colonizing army, bringing their wives and children with them. They seized the land from the Britons and distributed it amongst themselves. Among the Saxons the sense of kinship was very highly developed; nowadays few Englishmen could tell you the names of all their second-cousins, but with the Saxons sixth-cousins were regarded as

A Saxon Ox-plough.

members of the family, for whose welfare and good conduct the entire family group had a vague responsibility. Consequently the new settlements which sprang up all over the country were mostly peopled by family groups, consisting of possibly a score or so of households. Being in a conquered and hostile country the huts of such a group would often be built near together within a stockade or similar defence, and such a protected settlement was known as a *tun* : the word came later to be applied to larger collections of houses and passed into our language as ' town ', but it survived in its older sense as the -ton, which is such a common ending of place-names. Round the *tun* lay the great open fields in which, as we have seen, the crops of the settlers were grown, and a varying amount of pasture and woodland. To each household was assigned a quantity of land supposed to be sufficient for its support : in theory this quantity was a ' hide ', ' carucate ', or ' plough-land ', that is as much land as could be tilled every year with the great plough drawn by eight oxen, averaging roughly 120 acres : in practice it is pretty clear that there were varying grades of society, and that while the superior households obtained their plough-lands, a great many had to be content with a half or a quarter. Whatever the size of the allotment, it was not in a compact block, but was composed of strips scattered throughout the various fields. It was, however, the absolute property of the head of the household, to whom it had been granted—but only as head of the family ; he could not sell it or get rid of it, as that would injure the family ; on his death it would be divided between his sons.

We have thus traced the rise of the private ownership of land. But there were still great tracts of land unappropriated and therefore belonging vaguely to ' the people ', though probably no one could say whether ' the people ' meant the tribe, the nearest *tun*-dwellers, or any individual who chose to stake out a claim and work on it. The first period of armed colonization was followed by a period during which the settlers in each district established their position within their own borders ; the army leaders became kings, and the king with his *witan*, or council of wise men (warriors, priests, and experienced elders), became the acknowledged representative of the community. The land which had been distributed to the settlers remained the absolute property of the families to which it had been given, and was known as ' folk-land ', but the unappropriated land was con- sidered to be at the disposal of the king and his *witan*, and by them it was granted to individuals—usually nobles or priests. As such a grant was made by a ' book ', that is to say a written deed or charter, these estates were known as ' book-land ', and they were so completely the property of the man to whom they were given that he could sell them or give them to whom he chose. Thus there grew up a class of landed proprietors, who possessed more land than they required for the support of their households and cultivated it with the labour of slaves or of their poorer

The Manor Farmyard: c. 1460

The man and woman in the background are beating copper pans to make
the swarming bees (shown disproportionately large) settle down

neighbours. In various ways this wealthy class extended their influence; poorer men sought their protection for themselves and their lands, the king made them responsible for maintaining the law and collecting the taxes in particular districts, new villages grew up on their private estates and the villagers held their lands on condition of working on the landlord's farm. By the middle of the eleventh century the majority of English villages were practically owned by landlords who possessed a large part of the actual soil and extensive rights over the lands, and even over the persons, of the villagers.

The Normans found England divided up into vills—each containing a group of houses surrounded by the common corn-fields, grazing grounds, woods, and meadows, and each serving as a unit for purposes of law and taxation. To this Saxon organization they added the organization of the manor, which they brought with them from Normandy. As the Saxons had originally seized the land from the Britons, so now William the Conqueror seized all the land of England into his own hand and distributed the greater part of it to the nobles and warriors who came with him from France. They in turn gave estates to their friends and followers, who held them from the grantors as the latter held them from the king. These estates were formed into manors. In the manor-house dwelt the lord, or his representative, and there he held his court : it might be termed a court in three senses, for, as the manor-house was a farm as well as a dwelling, it would almost always possess a courtyard surrounded with farm buildings, and secondly, in a figurative sense, it might be styled a court as the lord might be called a king among his subjects, the tenants, but it is in the third and legal sense of a law-court that I have used the term. The possession of a court at which the business of the estate could be transacted and offences against its regulations punished was one of the marks of a manor. Round the house lay the enclosed fields of the ' demesne ' or home-farm, that portion of the estate which the lord kept in his own hands and cultivated with the aid of his tenants and servants : part of the demesne, however, often lay in the open fields, mingled with the strips belonging to the tenants. Of the remaining land, part was held by ' free tenants '—free men who were, in the eyes of the Law, on an equality with the lord, and might, indeed, themselves be lords of other manors : they usually paid money rents and rendered certain services, of which the most important was their attendance at the manor courts.

The rest of the land, usually the largest part, was held by ' unfree ' tenants. They were not slaves, but they were so much the property of their lord that they could be sold with their land, and while they certainly held land it would be equally true to say that the land held them—for they could not get rid of it or leave it without their lord's permission. These ' villeins ', that is men of the vill, held on an average from fifteen to forty acres, in return for which they had to work on their lord's demesne. In theory they could be turned out of their holdings at any moment, and also they could be compelled to work to an unlimited extent ; but in practice we find from the earliest times for which we have any details—the twelfth century—that the work due was fixed by the custom of the particular manor (whence villeins were commonly called ' customary tenants '), and that so long as these duties were performed the villein ran little risk of being ejected. A typical villein would have to work for his lord two or three days every week at whatever work was required ; he would be expected to plough or harrow about an acre or an acre and a half, to reap an acre of corn, mow a quarter of an acre of grass, or thrash two bushels of wheat or four of barley in the course of the day. Or he might be turned on to cart and spread manure, to collect reeds for thatching the buildings, to fetch salt from some place on the coast, or carry farm produce to market. The Knights Templars made the tenants of one of their Kentish manors dry and salt 5,000 herrings, and the monks of Battle Abbey had the cloth which they bought at the great Winchester fair brought to the abbey by some of the villeins on their manor of Appledram, half-way between Winchester and Battle. In addition to the regular week work there were extra demands upon the villein's time, especially during the busy season of harvest. It was very important to cut and carry the corn when the weather was favourable—so important that the Church even sanctioned harvesting work on Sunday—and, therefore, the villein would be required to put in several extra days at reaping, cocking, and carrying ; the lords so far admitted that this extra work was done by the goodwill of the tenants and at their own request rather than demanded of right that they called it ' boonwork ', and even ' love-boonwork ', and ' bederipe ' (which means reaping by request)—just as Tudor monarchs when they extorted loans called them ' benevolences '. ' Fine words butter no peas ', as our forefathers used to say, and the peasants probably cared little what their work was called, but they did appreciate the fact that as a rule they were given a good square meal at their harvest work—bread and cheese and beef, or a herring at least, and plenty of ale—though one stingy Bedfordshire landlord cut off the ale and made it a ' water-bederipe ', and ' hungry bede-ripes ' were not uncommon.

It might be thought that the villein, burdened with all this work upon his lord's land, would have no time to cultivate his own. But it is probable that all the labour due from him would not always be required, and even a full day's work seems usually to have ended at three o'clock, leaving him some time, though, as work started at daybreak, possibly not much inclination, to attend to his own affairs. Also, most householders would have a wife and sons, or younger brothers, who would help. Moreover, quite early in the history of the manorial system, a custom came in of compounding for labour services by money payments ; a villein might buy out all, or part, of his works by paying a penny or twopence for each day and the lord would then hire labourers. This freed the villein from continual calls upon his time ; it suited the lord, as he could get the labour when he most wanted it and the work of the hired men would be more likely to be satisfactory than the forced labour ; it was also good for the poorer inhabitants of the manor, the cottagers, who were thus able to earn money. Consequently by the middle of the four-teenth century a great part of these compulsory works (with the

A Harvest Scene: c. 1500
Below, boys throwing at a cock tied to a stick

exception of those required during the all-important harvest) had been converted into money payments. Then, in 1349, came the terrible Black Death, which swept away about a third of the population of England; labour became scarce and some lords of manors tried to revive the old work services. This was one of the causes of the Peasants' Rising of 1381; but although that rising collapsed, it was not found possible to go back to the old system; if compulsory labour had been grudging and half-hearted when it was regarded as part of the natural order of life, it would have been still worse when looked upon as a grievance. So the process of compounding for work-dues went on, and by the end of the Middle Ages, although much land was still said to be held 'in villenage' and its tenants were still called 'customary tenants', the distinction between free and unfree men had practically disappeared.

When a man acquired a piece of customary land, either by purchase or by inheritance, he had to appear at the manor court, take an oath of 'fealty', or loyalty, to the lord, and pay a fine (usually two years' rent); the account of his so doing and of his subsequent admission as a tenant, was written on the roll (of parchment) of the manor court and a copy of the entry was given to the tenant, who was thus said to hold 'by copy of court roll'. These copyhold tenures still exist,[1] though growing fewer every year, and sometimes prove to be unpleasant survivals of bygone times; for, as one of the incidents of such a tenure is that on the death of a tenant the lord of the manor has his 'best beast' as a 'heriot' (a kind of death duty), it may happen that on the death of a racing man his best race-horse will be seized because he happened to own some wretched little cottage with a cabbage-patch which is copyhold of some manor, and his unfortunate heirs will have either to lose the horse or ransom it for a sum many times the value of the cottage.

While on the subject of heirs it is worth while considering the question of the descent of land. The natural proceeding on the death of a landowner would be to divide his estate between his

---

[1] Since this was written copyhold tenure has been abolished by the new *Landed Property Act* (1925).

children—or in the Middle Ages between his sons, for in those unenlightened days girls were considered of very secondary importance. This was frequently done in very early times and continued to be the practice in Kent, where this special rule of land-holding was called ' gavelkind '. Elsewhere, with few exceptions, it became the custom, and, about the end of the twelfth century, the law, that the whole land should descend to one son. This unfair custom arose partly because in those days of large families the division of a property between the sons of successive generations would soon reduce a fair estate to a number of scraps and patches of land hardly worth owning, but mainly because under the feudal and manorial systems tenants owed valuable services to their lords, and while it was easy for a lord to enforce their performance upon a single tenant, it would be almost impossible to extort them in fractions from a score of descendants of the original tenant. It was, no doubt, through the influence of the lords that ' primogeniture '—the descent of land to the eldest son—became the general rule, because the eldest was most likely to be of an age to perform the necessary services at the death of his father. The alternative rule that the youngest son should inherit the land, which was the rule in some places, was justified from the tenant's point of view, because he was likely to be the last to remain at home after his elder brothers had set up for themselves. For some reason the law of equality held good in the case of women ; when there were only daughters their father's estate was divided evenly between them—so evenly that if there was only one dwelling-house on the estate it was divided, each coheir receiving certain rooms. There were a few exceptions to this rule, as for instance when the estate included a castle ; it would obviously be unsafe for it to be under divided control and it was therefore assigned entirely to one of the coheirs. Similarly, in 1291, when the succession to the throne of Scotland was disputed between the descendants of three coheirs (daughters of the brother of a former king), it was decided that the kingdom could not be divided. In actual practice the descent of land to one son was slightly modified by the fact that the dead man's cattle, money, and goods could be divided among the other sons. It would often be worth the elder brother's while to give his younger brothers part of his land in exchange for their cattle.

By a rather similar compromise important changes were brought about in the agricultural system. Tenants, as we have seen, held most of their land in small strips dotted about the open fields of the manor : after a time they began in many places to exchange some of these isolated strips for others adjoining one of their own strips, and in this way obtained compact blocks of land, which in time became separate enclosed fields. Also, during the fifteenth and early sixteenth centuries, when labour was scarce and wool was fetching a high price, many lords of manors found it paid better to give up growing corn and enclose as much as possible of their ground as grazing land for sheep, turning out the peasants, whose labour as ploughmen, reapers, and threshers they no longer required. So that ' the shepe, that were wont to be so meke and tame and so smal eaters ', says Sir Thomas More,

be become so greate devowerers and so wylde that they eate up and swallow downe the very men them selfes. They consume, destroye, and devoure whole fieldes, howses, and cities. For looke, in what partes of the realme doth growe the fynest and therefore dearest wool, there noblemen and gentlemen, yea, and certeyn abbottes—holy men no doubt—not contenting them selfes with the yearely revenues and profytes that were wont to growe to theyr forefathers and predecessours of their landes, leave no grounde for tillage ; they throwe downe houses ; they plucke down townes and leave nothing standynge but only the churche to be made a shepehowse. Therefore, that one covetous and unsatiable cormorant and very plague of his natyve countrey may inclose many thousand akers of grounde together within one pale or hedge, the husbandmen be thrust owte of their owne, or els either by fraude or by violent oppression they be put out of it, or by wronges and injuries they be so weried that they be compelled to sell all. By one meanes or by other, by hooke or crooke they must needes departe awaye, poore, wretched soules, men, women, husbands, wives, fatherlesse children, widowes, wofull mothers with their yong babes, and their whole houshold, smal

September habet dies xxx
Luna vero xxix

xvi	f	
v	g	Sancti Antonini martyris
xiii	b	
ii	c	
	d	
x	e	
	f	Natiuitas bte marie
xviii	g	
vii		Nicolai de tollentino cofessors
	b	
xv	c	Adriani martyris
iiii	d	
	e	Exaltatio s. crucis
xii	f	
i	g	Euphemie virginis et mar
		Festum sacrorum stigmatum
ix	b	beati Francisci d. ma
	c	
xvii	d	Eustachii et sociorum eius
vi	e	Mathei apli et euangeliste
	f	
xiiii	g	Lini pape et martyris
iii		

Sowing: c. 1500
A page of the Calendar for the month of September

in substance and muche in numbre, as husbandrye requireth manye handes. . . . For one shephearde or herdman is enoughe to eate up that grounde with cattel, to the occupying wherof aboute husbandrye many handes were requisite.'

So if we made a survey of a typical manor at the beginning and end of the Middle Ages, say in 1066 and 1566, we should see at the earlier date great stretches of ploughed land lying partly round the manor-house and partly in three great blocks round

A Village Scene. Soldiers plundering : 16th century.

the village. On this land we should see perhaps fifty or sixty men at work, ploughing, harrowing, sowing, digging, and so forth, while on the common there would be a few cattle in charge of a boy and a small flock of sheep watched by a couple of shepherds. At the later date cattle and sheep would still be grazing on the common, but round the manor-house we should now see green fields enclosed with hedges, some containing cattle but more sheep ; turning to the village we should find it surrounded by a sea of small hedged fields, some of which we can recognize, through their being divided up by strips of unploughed grass, as the last remnants of the common-fields, while many of the others have been turned into pasture for sheep : moreover,

we should now see barely twenty men at work upon the land.
If we look more closely at the village itself we see, at the earlier

*Shepherds : c. 1460. The seated shepherd is playing on the pipe ; both
have staves with weeding-spuds for digging up roots ; the dogs wear
spiked collars for defence against wolves.*

period, a cluster of hovels such as may still be seen in parts of
Ireland—one-storied buildings with mud walls and thatched

roofs, containing a single room ; the door stands always open to allow the pigs and chickens to wander in and out and also to let in light. If there are windows they will be unglazed, but may have wooden shutters; in winter there will be a wood fire burning in the middle of the earthen floor, and the smoke from it will find its way out through the door and windows—or more probably will not, but that does not matter, it is a healthy smell and helps to drown the more unpleasant odours of the hut even if it does make the eyes smart. All the hovels will be very much alike, and even the manor-house, though it contains three or four rooms, would probably be condemned by a modern county council inspector as unfit for human habitation. Five hundred years later some such hovels are still to be seen, but most of the houses are of timber and plaster and some of brick, two-storied buildings with several separate rooms and glass in many of the windows. There is now much greater difference between the houses, ranging from tiny cottages to roomy farm-houses with fire-places and chimneys, though the older inhabitants still regard these as new-fangled contraptions. It is easy to see that we have passed from an age of communal life to an age of individualism, from a time when few men were much better off than their neighbours and all worked side by side, to a time of greater inequality when half the village works under the other half.

In early days much of the cooking, at any rate in the summer, would be done over an outside fire, which was all right for roasting and boiling but not very convenient for baking. The lord of the manor would, therefore, usually establish a common bakehouse where the tenants could get their bread baked for a small charge. This was not pure benevolence on his part ; it was a source of revenue, and he not only permitted but compelled the villeins to use his ovens, though the custom died out in England much earlier than in France, where it was one of the grievances of the peasants at the time of the French Revolution. Similarly the lord compelled his tenants to grind their corn at his mill, and one of the great quarrels between the Abbot of St. Albans and his tenants was over his refusal to allow them to

Hand-mill

Water-mill with eel-traps

Windmill

Fourteenth-century Mills

use hand-mills in their houses. The Abbot was successful in maintaining his right and, as a sign of his victory, paved a court-yard with the millstones taken from the offenders—a memorial of his power which the townsmen destroyed during the rising of 1381. The early mills were worked by water-power, windmills being practically unknown in England before the beginning of the thirteenth century—a fact which gave additional value to the rivers and streams, apart from their importance as sources of water and of food, particularly of eels, of which great quantities were eaten in medieval times. For the use of the mill payment was made in kind, that is to say a certain proportion of the corn brought to be ground was kept for the owner of the mill, and the millers were notorious for their dishonesty. Court rolls are full of cases of millers taking more than their due share, and medieval popular literature is full of references to thievish millers. Chaucer, describing the miller among the Canterbury pilgrims, says, ' Wel coude he stele corn and profit thrice ', and of the miller of Trumpington he says, ' A theef he was, for-soth, of corn and mele, And that a sly, and using for to stele.'

One conspicuous feature of the village has not yet been alluded to—the church. Of the church as the centre of religious life something will be said in a later chapter, but there was not in the Middle Ages the same division between religious and everyday life as in later times, and the church was as much the centre of the social life of the peasantry as the manor-house was of their labouring life. It was the symbol of that equality in the eyes of God and in the future life, which made some amends for inequality in the eyes of the Law during this life. It represented the one power that was not afraid to stand up against kings and nobles, and might on occasion stand between those nobles and their poor subjects. The church was the meeting-place for the transaction of village business ; it often served as a bank or strong-room, parishioners depositing in the church chest their deeds and money, for which they had no place of safety in their own houses ; in the church chest also was kept a small fund for the relief, by gift or loan, of those suffering from sickness or misfortune. The labourer's holidays were associated with the church, for they were the holy-days or festivals of the saints, some of which—in particular the feast-day of the saint to whom the church was dedicated—were kept as ' wakes ' with feasting and merriment in the church and churchyard. There booths were set up for the sale of food and drink and other attractions— which was one of the ways in which fairs originated. The English have always been a nation of great eaters and wonderful drinkers, and as at the present day the favourite way of celebrating an event, honouring a distinguished person or raising money for any object is to give a dinner, so in medieval times our ancestors commemorated their saints by ' wakes ' and raised money for church expenses by ' church-ales '. These were feasts, held usually at Easter or Whitsun, for which the churchwardens brewed great quantities of ale, from malt supplied by the parishioners, and sold it at a considerable profit : they were, in principle, not unlike the refreshment stalls at church bazaars, where amiable ladies buy back the cakes which they have themselves contributed, but they were conducive to greater gaiety. An Elizabethan puritan, speaking of church-ales, which were still used in his day, says :

' The manner of them is thus. In certaine townes, where drunken Bacchus bears the sway, against Christmas, Easter, Whitsonday or some other time, the Church-wardens of every parish, with the consent of the whole parish, provide half a score or twenty quarters of mault, wherof some they buy out of the Church stock and some is given them of the parishioners them selves, every one conferring somewhat, according to his abilitie ; which mault, being made into very strong ale or beere, is sett to sale either in the Church or some other place assigned to that purpose. Then when this Huf-cap (as they call it) is set abroche, well is he that can get the soonest to it and spend the most at it ; for he that sitteth the closest to it and spends the moste at it, he is counted the godliest man of all the rest ; but who either cannot, for pinching povertie, or otherwise wil not stick to it, he is counted one destitute bothe of vertue and godlynes. In so much as you shall have many poor men make hard shift for money to spend therat, for they are perswaded it is meritorious and a good service to God.'

The officers of the manor were not slow to take a hint from the officers of the church ; the stewards and bailiffs instituted ' scot-ales '. They went round at harvest-time and compelled the poor peasants to give them part of their scanty store of grain to be converted into malt, and when this had been brewed into ale they compelled the villagers to buy it. Laws were passed against ' scot-ales ', but with little effect. In picturing the life of the medieval peasant one must always bear in mind the presence of these lesser officials with their power to render the peasant's life a burden to him. Men of peasant birth themselves, raised to a little brief authority over their fellows, they were in the position of sergeants in a regiment or prefects in a school, able to make things very unpleasant for their subordinates, unless their superior officers and masters kept a sharp eye on them. When Edward I, at the beginning of his reign, ordered a general inquiry into the state of the kingdom, the returns from all parts of the country were full of complaints against the bailiffs and other officials—mostly extortion of money by threats, but sometimes illegal imprisonment and torture, while in Yorkshire the bailiff of the Earl of Lincoln had done ' many acts of oppression, robbery, and injuries beyond belief ', and the steward of Earl Warenne had committed ' innumerable devilish acts of oppression '.

The steward was the representative of the lord of the manor, and usually responsible for a number of manors. He had to hold the courts and was, therefore, bound to have some knowledge of law ; it was his duty to know how much each manor ought to produce, and to keep a general eye to his lord's interests. Under him was the bailiff, who had to have a good knowledge of agriculture, so that he did not have constantly to be asking the steward or lord for instructions. It was his duty to oversee the working of the manor farm in general and to keep watch on the other servants. The servants included the hayward, who was responsible for the proper keeping of the meadows, hedges, and woods, the foreman of the mowers, the cowherd, swineherd, and shepherd, the dairymaid, who had charge also of the poultry, and, most important of all, the reeve. The reeve, who was elected by the villeins from their own number, was responsible for the actual running of the farm, his duties overlapping with those of the bailiff. He had to see that the servants were up and the ploughs yoked betimes in the morning, that the live stock were properly cared for, the corn well threshed and none of it stolen, that the women employed in the dairy did not take away any cheese or butter, and that the herdsmen did not go off to taverns or fairs or wrestling-matches. Chaucer's reeve of

Reapers and the Reeve : c. 1300.

Norfolk, who brought up the rear of the cavalcade of pilgrims, knew his business thoroughly :

> Wel wiste he by the drought and by the reyn
> The yeelding of his seed and of his greyn.
> His lordes sheep, his cattle, his dayerie,
> His swyn, his hors, his store and his poultrie,
> Was wholly in this reeves governynge . . .
> Ther was ne baylyf, herde ne other hyne [1]
> That he ne knewe his sleight and his covyne ; [2]
> They were adread of him as of the deth.

No small job had the reeve, to know all the operations of farming, though there are foolish townsfolk nowadays who think that farming is unskilled labour. The farmer's year began in

---

[1] farm-servant.   [2] deceitful tricks.

September, as soon as the harvest had been carried. Then the land had to be ploughed and sown with winter wheat, or with rye if the land was too light and sandy for wheat. The plough consisted of two heavy beams, one above the other, connected by vertical struts ; the lower beam had at its front end a pointed curved piece of iron, the share, to cut the earth and turn it aside, and in front of the share a knife-like piece of iron, the coulter, to start the cut or furrow ; at the hinder end were two wooden uprights, both fastened into the lower beam, and that on the left also fastened to the end of the upper beam ; these formed the tail, or plough-start, by which the ploughman guided it. The heavy Saxon plough was drawn by eight oxen, but lighter ploughs were used with four, or even two, oxen, yoked in pairs :

' The ploughman's art consisteth herein, that he drive the yoked oxen evenly, neither smiting nor pricking or grieving them. Such men should not be melancholy nor wrathful but cheerful, lively, and full of song, that by their melody and song the oxen may in a manner rejoice in their labour. Such a ploughman should bring the fodder with his own hands, and love his oxen and sleep with them by night, tickling and combing and rubbing them with straw ; keeping them well in all respects and guarding their forage from theft.'

Sometimes horses were used for ploughing, but they were more expensive, as they required better feeding, and had to be constantly re-shod, and although they could go faster, the medieval ploughman usually refused to be hurried and kept them back to the pace of oxen. When the corn had been sown it had to be covered by harrowing. The harrow was a large and very heavy grid or lattice of thick oaken bars crossing one another at right-angles, furnished with rows of wooden teeth projecting downwards. This was slowly dragged across the field by oxen, breaking up the clods and so covering the seed.

At Michaelmas, in a good season, the woods would be full of ' mast ', that is to say, acorns and beech-nuts, an excellent food for pigs, so the pigs would be turned into the woods to feed. During November there would be more ploughing, to prepare the land for spring sowing, and most of the oxen would be slaughtered

Sowing and Harrowing: c. 1416

The figure with a bow is a scarecrow. The building in the background
is the Palace of the Louvre, at Paris

and salted down, as it was difficult to keep much live stock through the winter, hay being the only food available, the roots and artificial cakes now used being unknown. During December little could be done outside, but the threshers were busy in the barns beating the grain out of the ears of corn with their flails— wooden clubs fastened by leathern thongs to the end of poles. In January the cows would be calving, and during this month and February hedges and ditches had to be seen to and peas and beans, for cattle food, could be sown. March was a busy month, the time of sowing oats, rye, and especially barley, which was, next to wheat, the most important crop, as it was used for malt for making the ale of which our ancestors drank immense quantities. April was the busiest time for the dairy, making butter and cheese, for which in early times sheep's milk was preferred. Hemp and flax—important in those days when housewives spun and wove their own linen—had now to be sown. In May the fallow ground had to be ploughed over, and in June the corn required weeding and sheep were to be washed and sheared. By the beginning of July the hay should be mown, and towards the end of that month and during August the corn should be ripe and harvest in full swing, at the end of which the labourers might sit down to their harvest feast and regale themselves on goose and strong ale before starting upon another year.

Threshing : 15th century.

III

TOWN LIFE

THE difference between a town and a village is one of quantity rather than quality, of size rather than nature. There are places which are obviously towns and others which are equally clearly villages, but we most of us know places whose inhabitants proudly refer to them as towns and are much offended when strangers incautiously refer to them as villages. In the Middle Ages it is still more difficult to draw any distinct line between the two, as even the larger towns had many of the qualities of villages. Possibly at the present time the possession of sufficient shops to satisfy the ordinary needs of civilized life might be held to be the test of a town, and in the same way the existence in a medieval community of a certain number of tradesmen, persons who did not live solely by agriculture, was the mark of a town. We have seen that villages grew up by the settlement of a number of households, often connected by family ties, living together for purposes of protection ; and this same motive of mutual protection was probably the first cause of towns. In very early days the wandering British tribes had fortified positions, usually on hill-tops, surrounded by deep ditches and high banks, within which the scattered communities of the tribe could retire during periods of war or invasion. As life became more settled and villages grew up, the fortified village of the chief of the tribe, the centre of such government as existed, tended to become larger and more important than the others and probably still retained its character of a place of refuge in time of danger. The Romans encouraged the growth of these tribal towns and built others. Being a methodical race, they laid out their towns on neat mathematical lines ; one main street ran north and south, another east and west, cutting the first at the centre of the town ; other streets ran parallel to these two, dividing the whole town up into a series of rectangular blocks, one block—at the crossing of the main streets—being given up to the market-place, magis-

trates' court and town offices. Connected with one another by
the excellent roads for which the Romans were famous, these
towns became centres of trade and wealth.

The Saxons mistrusted walled cities ; their gods were the gods
of the open country, they felt ill at ease shut up within walls ;
so they sacked the towns and left them desolate, settling outside
in the fields. Even London appears to have been deserted for
a while. But not many generations passed before they too began
to see the advantages of town life ; once more it was the need for
protection that brought about the change, and this is shown by
the name given to certain towns—' burhs ' or ' boroughs ', which
means fortified places of security. As the country settlements,
the ' tuns ', are commemorated in place-names—Islington,
Preston, Southampton, and so forth—so are the boroughs in
names like Canterbury, Aylesbury and Peterborough, and when
the Saxons began to occupy the Roman walled towns they
attached to them their version of the Latin word *castrum* (a fortress) and produced such names as Chester, Lancaster, Gloucester,
and Chichester.

Boroughs, then, began as places of refuge and defence for the
districts of which they were the centres ; and their importance
was such that one of the three duties imposed upon all freemen
who held land was the upkeep of these fortifications—the other
two being military service and the repair of bridges. At the time
of the Domesday Survey (1086) we find that in certain boroughs,
such as Oxford, there were houses belonging to manors in different
parts of the county, the owners of which were responsible for the
defence of a certain portion of the town wall. (This wall was not
necessarily of stone ; more often it would be an earthen bank
with a stockade ; at Bridgenorth, for instance, in Shropshire—
a district constantly troubled by Welsh border raids—the wooden
defences of the town were only replaced by a stone wall in the
early years of Henry III, and throughout the thirteenth and
fourteenth centuries we find important towns licensed to raise
money to build stone walls.) These houses would be used in time
of war by such inhabitants of the manors as retired within the

A Street in the Fifteenth Century
An author, in travelling dress, presents a copy of his book to a noble

borough for safety or on garrison duty ; in time of peace they might be let or might be used by the manorial tenants who came in to buy and sell. For the boroughs soon began to be centres for the disposal of the surplus produce of the farms, and the security which they afforded soon attracted merchants, traders, and craftsmen of all kinds. The borough, therefore, was both a military and a trading centre, and as life became more peaceful and secure, new towns grew up purely for trading purposes and with little or no idea of defence.

The question now arises, why important towns should have grown up in the particular positions in which they did ? In answering this we must be careful to distinguish between cause and effect ; for instance, if we find a castle and a town together, the castle may have been built to control an existing town—as at Norwich, London, and many other places—or the town may have sprung up round the castle, as at Berkhampsted and many of the towns of the Welsh borders. There is a story of a pious friar, who, preaching on the goodness of Providence, bade his hearers observe how Providence almost always caused a river to run through large towns, to the great benefit of the inhabitants. Had he been as wise as he was pious it might have occurred to him that the rivers had got there first and that the towns had been built upon their banks because of the convenience of the position. Accessibility is one of the most important qualifications for a town site. Good harbours on the sea-coast led to the rise of such towns as Southampton, Dover, Boston, and Plymouth ; and the silting up of their harbours in the sixteenth century impoverished Chester and reduced Rye and Winchelsea from prosperous boroughs to insignificant country towns. Navigable rivers were even better sites. London, which started as the port for the great British city of Verulamium (where St. Albans now stands), owed its importance to the fact that it was the lowest point at which the Thames was bridged ; ships from the coast towns and from foreign lands could come up the river to this point, while the upper river and the roads which ran to the bridge brought merchandise and purchasers from the inland parts of the country.

In the same way Bristol grew up round the bridge across the
Avon and Norwich at the head of the navigable Yare. Even

Market Stalls: 1460.

Inside the gate is a money-changer's stall.

arther inland the rivers influenced the growth of towns; the
ords and bridges attracted the roads and traffic and became the
natural sites for trading towns, as we may see from such names as
Oxford and Cambridge. So too the junctions of roads; Winchester

was the meeting-place of six ancient roads; Salisbury, Cirencester and Huntingdon are other instances of towns of similar origin.

Any cause that would attract to a particular spot visitors with wants to be supplied and money to pay for their requirements would also attract dealers, eager to supply those wants and obtain that money. Therefore the neighbourhood of a great monastery, which was both a centre of pilgrimage and a sort of hotel for travellers, frequently developed into a town, as for instance, St. Albans, Bury St. Edmunds, and Peterborough. Sometimes there were special causes peculiar to the one place. Bath owed its existence to the hot springs which, from Roman times to the present day, have been visited by sufferers from rheumatism; Yarmouth was nothing but a collection of sand-banks, where the fishermen of the Cinque Ports spread their nets and smoked their herrings, until men came to buy herrings, to barter goods with the Portsmen and to join in the fishery. There were also towns deliberately founded by individuals. The port of Lynn was established by Bishop Herbert of Norwich in about 1100 on ground which he had reclaimed from the marshes: that of Kingston-on-Hull (now known as Hull) was founded, as its name implied, by King Edward I, who recognized the possibilities of the site. The same king, when the sea began to make inroads on the flourishing seaport of Winchelsea, laid out the town afresh on a neighbouring cliff and removed thither the inhabitants of the old town. This new Winchelsea was laid out in rectangular blocks, like an ancient Roman or a modern American city, and a similar plan was followed at an earlier date in Ludlow and other towns on the Welsh border, but generally the arrangement of a medieval town was haphazard and irregular.

The towns that during the Middle Ages deserve that name as distinguishing them from what were merely larger villages are those called boroughs. We have seen that originally this term meant a fortified place, but after the Norman Conquest it came to mean a town whose inhabitants possessed certain privileges and could act as a single body instead of as separate individuals. At the present time the London County Council consists of a large

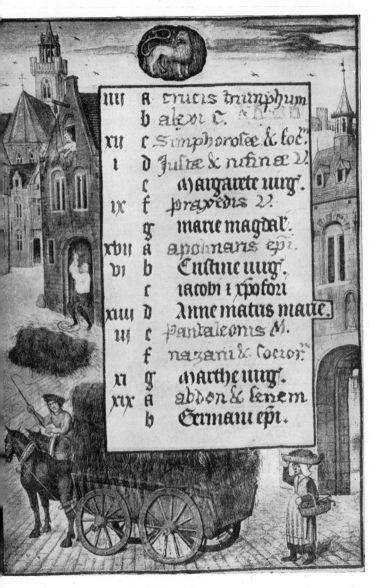

iiii   A   crucis triumphum
       b   alexi c.
xij   c   simphorose & soc.
i   d   Juste & rufine V.
       e   margarete uirg.
ix   f   praxedis V.
       g   marie magdal.
xvij   a   apolinaris epi.
vi   b   Cristine uirg.
       c   iacobi t xpofori
xiiij   d   Anne matris marie.
iij   e   pantaleonis M.
       f   nazarii & socior.
xi   g   marthe uirg.
xix   a   abdon & senem
       b   Germani epi.

A Street Scene

From a fifteenth-century calendar

number of persons who act as one whole ; when we say that the London County Council has passed such and such regulations, we do not think of the individual councillors but of an imaginary body which expresses the general opinion of those councillors. So when we say that ' the borough of Leicester ' passed certain by-laws, or provided so many soldiers, or owed the king so much money, we are speaking of an imaginary personification of the townsfolk of Leicester. A borough can act as an individual, but it ' has no soul to be saved and no body to be kicked ' ; it can break the law but it cannot be imprisoned, and if it is fined the money will have to be raised from the separate burgesses and it is not very easy to say who is responsible for payment.

Some towns were already boroughs at the time of the Norman Conquest ; many others, which at that time were manorial vills, differing little from the manors described in the last chapter, became boroughs during the twelfth and thirteenth centuries by obtaining charters from their lords, who required money for the crusades or other purposes, and were glad to sell part of their rights to the townsmen. Sometimes the manorial lord was the king, sometimes a noble (the Earl of Derby made Higham Ferrers a borough in 1251, and Bolton, in Lancashire, in 1253), and sometimes a monastery. This last class, the monastic lords, were the least willing to allow their towns to become boroughs and the most grudging in the granting of privileges, so that in such places as St. Albans, Bury St. Edmunds, Dunstaple, and Norwich there were continual quarrels between the monks and the townsmen, flaring up occasionally into such riots as that of 1270, in which the cathedral church of Norwich was burnt. When a manorial vill became a free borough it naturally did not lose its agricultural characteristics at once ; we are not surprised to find that the burgesses of little country towns like Steyning in Sussex or Dunster in Somerset (where the charter gave the burgesses leave to kill rabbits that damaged their gardens) remained peasants ; but it is more surprising to find an important and ancient town like Coventry or Leicester practically sur-rounded by its three great ' open fields ' and the burgesses of such

Open Fields round Cambridge

Although these views were drawn late in the 17th century they are typical of medieval conditions, showing the great fields undivided by hedges, and the sheep pastured on the reaped fields

places as Norwich and Oxford insisting on their pasturage rights, which rights the freemen of Oxford retain to this day. It is still more astonishing to any one whose idea of a town is such a place as Birmingham, Middlesborough or Leeds, to know that in the Middle Ages the city law-court of London ceased to sit during the harvest season, that a law was passed in 1388 by which all craftsmen whose work at their own trade was not urgently required must help with the harvest, and that even in the sixteenth century weavers at Norwich, the third most wealthy city in England, had to leave their looms and go harvesting. There was an agricultural element in all medieval towns ; even within the city walls London was full of gardens, and constant orders had to be issued against allowing pigs to wander about the streets. But although some burgesses were farm labourers they were not serfs or villeins but free men ; if a villein could escape into a town and remain there as a burgess for a year and a day without being claimed by his master he became free.

All the burgesses were free, all bore their share in the responsibilities of the town, as ratepayers do nowadays, and all were at first equal. They all met together from time to time to discuss questions of general policy and by their shouts of ' Yea, yea ! ' or ' Nay, nay ! ' such questions were decided. In particular they met once a year to elect their town council of twelve or twenty-four men with, at their head, a reeve, provost, bailiff, or mayor. By whichever title he was known, this official was the representative of the town ; his post though honourable was full of responsibility, but if he refused to accept it he would be heavily fined and in certain towns the community might even go and pull down his house. He acted as chief magistrate and presided over the borough court, and with the aid of his council drew up regulations for the government of the town. At first such regulations had to be agreed to by all the burgesses, but as time went on the population of the towns increased, the merchants and leading tradesmen became more wealthy, and we find the burgesses classified as superior, middle, and inferior. No exact line can be drawn between these classes, but the difference would be visible when the military forces of the town were called up, for by the Assize of Arms all who had property above a certain amount had to appear fully armed and mounted, those less well off had a lighter equipment and no horses, while the poorest class wore no defensive armour and carried bows, pitchforks, clubs, or whatever weapons they could obtain. The wealthy class gradually usurped all the power, and often used it to tax their poorer brethren unfairly. For instance, at Lynn in 1305 rates which ought not to have been levied without the unanimous consent of the community were extorted from the poorer class, and instead of being used for repairs to the town walls and streets were misappropriated. From Oxford, Cambridge, York, and Lincoln come bitter complaints of similar oppression about the same time, and when Bristol was fined £500 for some offence the king had specially to order that the money should be raised in such a way that the rich should not escape.

Trade being the distinguishing mark of a town, as opposed to a village, equality of trading rights was an important privilege of the townsmen. All the burgesses—or, at any rate, all members of the Gild Merchant, which was a society, existing in every large town,[1] to which originally all persons engaged in trade within the town belonged (though, as time went on, the poorer classes were squeezed out of the gild)—had the right to buy and sell within the borough without paying toll. Equality was carried still farther in some places, where collective bargaining prevailed —that is to say, any gildsman could claim to share in another gildsman's purchase ; if one member of the gild bought any goods wholesale to be sold retail, any other member who was present could insist upon taking part in the deal. This prevented any one getting a monopoly or unfair share of any particular trade. In the same way attempts to push the sale of goods were discouraged as unfair to the less enterprising traders, who, as members of the same community had an equal right to make a living. The community was also protected from competition from outside

[1] London and Norwich were practically the only large towns without Gilds Merchant.

by the levying of tolls on goods bought or sold by 'foreign' traders. Foreign in this case meant a man from any place outside the borough ; a man from Nottingham was as much ' a foreigner ' in Norwich as a man from Venice or Bordeaux ; he was outside (Latin—*foris*) the privileged community.

In the Middle Ages the idea of nationality was weak compared with the idea of citizenship. Now a man from Durham or from Exeter will proudly proclaim himself an Englishman, but in those days he would be more likely to boast, with St. Paul, that he was ' a citizen of no mean city '. Every borough was a little state, jealous of all rivals ; for two hundred years the men of Yarmouth carried on a quarrel with the confederacy of Sussex and Kentish ports known as the Cinque Ports—a quarrel which constantly flamed into actual warfare, in which hundreds of lives were lost ; the Cinque Ports also found time to attack their rivals of Portsmouth and Fowey, while the men of Yarmouth marched in arms against the neighbouring town of Gorleston. If the inland towns were less violent in their methods, they were always on the watch to protect their privileges against outsiders. Occasionally an exception would be made in favour of special towns ; Nottingham made treaties with Derby and Coventry, as did Southampton with Winchester and Salisbury, by which each released the other's burgesses from payment of tolls, and in the same way London and Norwich made special arrangements for trading facilities with the French towns of Amiens, Corbeil, and Nesle, and the great trading confederacy of ports on the North Sea and Baltic, known as the Hanseatic League, had special privileges in London.

While ' foreigners ' were thus usually made to pay if they came into the town to trade, and were not allowed to settle in the town unless they joined the Gild Merchant, these restrictions might be relaxed for special reasons for the benefit of the community. In the sixteenth century, when Chester had become very impoverished, proclamation was made that any one who could teach the art of making the finer qualities of cloth might come and carry on their trade freely. In the same city, when the bakers went on strike because they were not allowed to raise the price of bread, the mayor proclaimed that any one might bring bread into the city for sale. This was typical of the attitude of the authorities towards any attempt at profiteering ; they regarded the trades-man as the servant of the community, deserving a reasonable profit but by no means to be allowed an excessive one. When the Chester butchers struck for higher prices the mayor promptly clapped the lot of them in prison, where, as it was very hot weather and they were very crowded, they had a most un-pleasant time and soon repented of their misdeeds.

The borough courts were kept pretty busy with trade offences, for there were few ways of earning a dishonest penny that the medieval tradesman did not try. The prize for perverse ingenuity may perhaps be awarded to certain London bakers ; when their customers brought dough in to be baked they would put it down on the counter before making it into loaves, and a small boy hidden under the counter would open a little trap-door and remove a quantity of the dough before the customer's very eyes. Com-pared with such a trick the use of false weights and bad materials, passing off gilded copper as gold and selling shoddy goods at night by the dim light of flickering tapers, were clumsy devices. The offenders paid the penalty of their misdeeds by fines and imprisonment, or had to sit with their feet in the stocks or stand with their head and hands in the pillory, exposed to the derision of the crowd. Sometimes an attempt would be made to make the punishment fit the crime ; a dealer who had sold bad wine was compelled to drink some of it and had the rest poured over his head ; a man who had tapped a public water-supply for his own use was led through the streets with a leaky bucket, constantly refilled, on his head ; and the seller of bad meat had not only to stand in the pillory but had his meat burnt in front of him, where he would get the full benefit of the smell. Constant offenders were the bakers, whose loaves seem usually to have been under weight, and the brewers, who consistently broke the regulations as to measures and price of ale. Almost every medieval poem on town life has some allusion to the fraudulent bakers and brewers, and in one of the popular religious plays on ' The Harrowing of

Hell ', when all the souls are released the Devil begs to be allowed to keep one and is finally given the soul of a brewer—a touch of humour which would certainly appeal to the audience. So, also, the author of *Piers Plowman*, in the reign of Richard II, writes :

> Women that bake and brew, butchers and cooks,
> They are the people that harm the poor,
> They harm the poor who can but buy in pennyworths,
> And privily and oft they poison them.

A Fraudulent Baker : 1293.

On the left he is putting a small loaf into the oven ; on the right he is being drawn through the streets on a hurdle, with his light-weight loaf hung round his neck.

> They grow rich by retailing what the poor should eat ;
> They buy houses, they become landlords.
> If they sold honestly they would not build so high
> Nor buy their tenements.
> Mayors and their officers, the king's go-betweens
> Between the king and the commons to keep the laws,
> They should punish these in pillories and stocks.

The brewers, it may be observed, were mostly women, and we must not think of great breweries, on the modern lines, sending their drays round to the taverns. Every tavern brewed its own ale and after every brew put out its ' ale-stake ', which was a pole with a branch or bush of leaves at the end. These ale-stakes were sometimes so long and heavy that they injured the fronts of the houses to which they were attached and were dangerous to persons riding through the narrow streets, so that in London they were not allowed to be more than seven feet in length. In every division of the town there were officials known as ale-conners or ale-tasters, whose duty it was when a stake was put out to go and test the ale. If it was not good the whole brew would be forfeited and the tavern might even be closed ; but if it was satisfactory the tavern-keeper could proceed to sell it and might well hope to derive a thriving trade, for there were

A Tavern with its Ale-stake : c. 1340.

always plenty of customers where the ale was good. In the fourteenth-century poem of *Piers Plowman* we have a little picture in words of a London tavern and its customers : Glutton, repenting of his sins, starts off to go to church, but unfortunately meets Betty the brewster, who tells him that she has good ale and asks him to taste it :

> Then in goes Glutton, and great oaths welcomed him.
> Cis the sempstress sat on the bench,
> Walt the gamekeeper and his wife—drunk ;
> Tom the tinker and two of his 'prentices,
> Hick the hackneyman, Hogg the needler,
> Clarice of Cock Lane and the parish clerk ;
> Parson Piers of Pray-to-God and Pernel the Flemish woman,
> Daw the ditcher and a dozen more of them ;
> A fiddler, a ratter and a Cheapside scavenger,
> A ropemaker, a lackey, and Rose the retailer,
> A watchman and a hermit and the Tyburn hangman ;

Godfrey the garlic-seller and Griffin the Welshman,
All early in the morning welcomed Glutton gladly
To try the good ale.
There was laughing and chattering and ' Pass the cup round ',
Bargains and toasts and songs, and so they sat till evensong,
And Glutton had gulped down a gallon and a gill.
He could neither step nor stand till he had his staff ;
Then he 'gan walk like a blind singer's dog,
Now to this side, now to that, and sometimes backward,
Like a man who lays lines to catch wild birds ;
And when he drew to the doorstep, then his eyes grew dim,
He stumbled on the threshold and fell flat on the floor.

This is not a very pretty picture, but it is true to life. William Fitz-Stephen in his account of London, written in the twelfth century, names ' the immoderate drinking of fools ' as one of the two plagues from which the city suffered, and the records of coroners' inquests show how many deaths occurred through accidents and quarrels arising out of drunkenness.

The account of Fitz-Stephen, just referred to, is the earliest and almost the only medieval description of a town. He begins by praising the situation of London and the excellence of its climate. London, it must be remembered, in medieval times was what is now known as ' the City '—the district within the walls, extending from the Tower on the east to Ludgate on the west and bounded on the north by Holborn and on the south by the river. At the end of the fourteenth century it had a population of only about 35,000, and even so it was more than three times as big as York, while Bristol with 9,500, Coventry with 7,000, and Norwich with 6,000 were probably the only towns in England with more than 5,000 inhabitants. In Fitz-Stephen's time the population would have been rather less, yet there were within the walls 136 parish churches, besides St. Paul's Cathedral and 13 monasteries. This lavish provision of churches was a feature of ancient towns ; Norwich had its cathedral and over 50 churches, Cambridge had 15, and even so small a town as Lewes had eight. All round the city lay gardens, pastures, and fertile cornfields, and beyond them the forest, in which the

Interior of a Tavern: c. 1500.

Arrival of officials to test the ale and collect excise duties. The clerk on the left carries a knife and two sticks, which are either measures for gauging casks or long 'tally' sticks on which accounts were kept by means of notches; his companion has a money-bag and a number of short tallies, and the lady behind the bar is cutting another tally

citizens had the right of hunting stags and boars and lesser game. Within the walls craftsmen of every kind had their shops, each trade keeping as a rule to its own street or district, in accordance with the general custom in early times, so that corn was for sale on Cornhill, fish in Fish Street, the metal-workers congregated in Lothbury, the goldsmiths in Cheapside, and the drapers in what is now Cannon Street. On the river bank, near the wine wharves, were the cook-shops, where every variety of fish, flesh, and fowl, roast meat, baked meat, stew, and pasty was ever preparing. Hither ran the servants of those upon whose empty larders unexpected guests had descended ; here was store sufficient to satisfy an army of knights or a band of pilgrims ; here an epicure might call for sturgeon, woodcock, or ortolan ; and here—as Fitz-Stephen does not tell us, but as we learn from other records—the purchaser of a meat-pie ran a considerable risk of being poisoned with bad meat. Cooks' Row must have been a busy, smelly scene, and a noisy one with the salesmen crying their wares ; for in *Piers Plowman* we read how :

> Cooks and their men were crying ' Pies hot, all hot,
> Good pork, good goose ; come, come and dine '.
> Taverners told the same tale, ' A drink of wine for nothing,
> White wine, red wine, to wash the roast meat down.'

Medieval London was a gay, busy, prosperous city, with ships of all nations loading and unloading at the riverside, tradesmen calling their wares, and crowds buying and bargaining at the stalls and open shop-windows. From time to time the crowd would have to scatter to make way for a procession of priests or the mounted retinue of some great lord. On occasion, too, business would be suspended and the streets thronged with people to watch the king ride by in state, going to be crowned at Westminster Abbey or returning from the wars. At such times the houses would be hung with silks and brightly coloured cloths, in the open spaces would be built up stages, covered with decoration, on which were fair ladies in beautiful dresses, representing Virtues, Sciences, or other allegorical figures, who would recite Latin verses of a moral but otherwise uninteresting nature for the king's benefit. In the king's procession would ride his nobles, gorgeous in silks and velvet, their very horses covered with cloth-of-gold, the mayor and aldermen in scarlet, and four or five hundred citizens, all wearing the same colours.

A Royal Procession: c. 1375.
An escort of 'wiffelers', or policemen, with clubs.

'Of triumphant shewes made by the citizens of London, ye may read in the yere 1236, Andrew Bockwell then being Maior, how Helianor daughter to Raymond Earle of Provance, riding hrough the Citie towardes Westminster, there to be crowned Queene of England, the Citie was adorned with silkes, and in the ight with lamps, cressets and other lights without number, esides many pageants and straunge devises there presented. he Citizens also rode to meet the King and Queene, clothed in ong garments embroidered about with gold and silks of diverse colours, their horses gallantly trapped, to the number of 360, every man bearing a cup of gold or silver in his hand, and the king's trumpetters sounding before them.'

Though such a pageant as a coronation occurred but rarely, there was every year the excitement of ' the marching watch ' on the night of Midsummer Eve, when the constables and police patrols assembled fully armed and marched through the principal streets, headed by the mayor and aldermen and attended by torch-bearers, each with a straw hat bearing the badge of his company or ward, archers, drums and fifes, and morris dancers ; bonfires blazed in the streets and the houses were gay with garlands and bright with lamps.

The full splendour of the Midsummer Watch belongs, it is true, to the later period of the Middle Ages, but life in London was far from dull even in the twelfth century. Fitz-Stephen tells of the weekly excitement of the horsefair held outside the city walls on the flat fields of Smithfield ; every one was there, come to buy, to sell, or to look on—and there were horses to suit all wants— at least if you took their owners' word. Here were ambling nags for priests or ladies to ride, unbroken colts, of whose heels a man had better beware, stately chargers, sturdy pack-horses, mares with their foals, cart-horses, horses innumerable. At a sudden shouting the crowd would hastily part, leaving a clear course, down which the chargers thundered in a mad race, urged on by the cries of their boy jockeys. On holidays the boys and young men would play at tilting, wrestling, football, or other games of ball, not only in the fields but in the streets, though as time went on efforts were made to suppress street games ; wrestling was forbidden in St. Paul's churchyard, ' bars ', or ' prisoner's base ', and games that involved the annoyance of passers-by were prohibited in Westminster when parliament was sitting, and football was constantly denounced, with good reason as it was not an orderly game with a fixed number of players, definite rules, and regular goals, but a wild struggle between opposing parties to force the ball through the streets from one end of the town to the other, frequently resulting in broken legs

Bowls and quoits, played down the streets, doubtless relieved life of its monotony, but also occasionally relieved an unwary pedestrian of his life altogether, and were, therefore, not en-couraged in towns. In the winter, when the marshes were covered with ice, the young men would fasten to their feet rough skates made of the leg-bones of animals, and, propelling themselves with iron-shod poles, shoot across the ice, tilting at one another, to the breaking of many heads and limbs. Rough sport; but it was, in our eyes, a rough and brutal age, and we may regard their readiness to risk wounds and injuries for fun as some set-off against their readiness to inflict cruelty on animals for the same purpose, as shown in their fondness for baiting bulls and bears — worrying them to death with dogs—cock-fighting, and, the particular amusement of schoolboys, throwing sticks at a cock tied by the leg to a post.

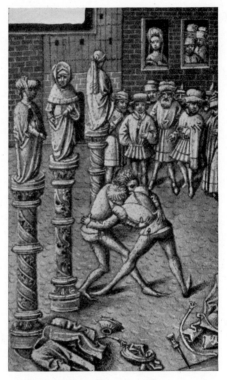

Wrestling : c. 1460.

Yet it must not be thought that our ancestors were insensible to gentler influences.

' In the month of May, namely on Mayday in the morning, every man, except impediment, would walke into the sweete meadows and greene woods, there to rejoyce their spirites with the beauty and savour of sweete flowers and with the harmony of birds praysing God in their kind. And for example hereof Edward Hall hath note that Henry the eight in the seventh yeare of his reign on Mayday in the morning, with the Queene Katheren his wife, accompanied with many Lords and Ladies rode a maying from Greenwich to the high ground of Shooters hill, where as they passed by the way they espied a companie of tall yeomen, cloathed all in greene, with greene hoodes, and with bowes and arrowes, to the number of 200. One, being their chieftaine, was called Robin Hoode, who desired the King and Queene with their retinue to enter the greene wood, where, in harbours made of boughs and decked with flowers, they were set and served plentifully with venison and wine by Robin Hoode and his meynie.'

Moreover, the various parishes had their mayings, ' and did fetch in Maypoles, with diverse warlike shewes, with good archers Morice dauncers, and other devices for pastimes all the day long And towards the evening they had stage playes and bonfiers in the streetes '. Of all these may-poles the greatest was the tall shaft set up before the church which to this day is known as St. Andrew Undershaft.

Such, then, was London or any other medieval city ; a self centred community, suspicious of a stranger and quite ready to ' heave half a brick at him ' (in 1421 the authorities at Coventry had to give orders ' that no man throw ne cast at no straunge man ne skorn hym '), proud of its privileges and inclined to rate its mayor somewhat above the king, anxious as a body to see fair play for all its members, but quite ready as individuals to take advantage of a neighbour ; a hard-working community with no mercy for ' big beggars that will not work well to get their living ', but tolerant towards the impotent and needy, and always ready for simple enjoyment in the shape of a show or a feast. The two great blots on town life which Fitz-Stephen noted were the moral one of drunkenness and the physical one of fire. The narrow streets, with their houses built of wood and covered with thatch, burnt with terrible ease and completeness In 1132 the greater part of London was burnt in a fire which

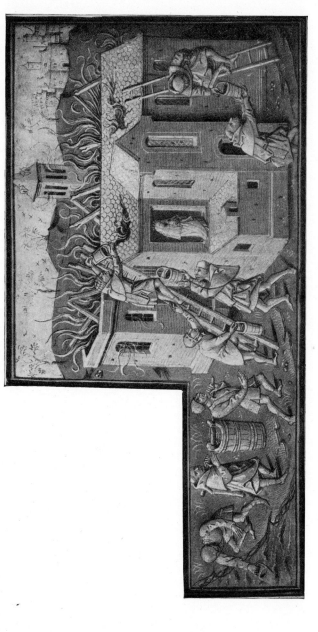

A Fire: c. 1460

started in the house of Gilbert Becket, father of the famous
Thomas Becket; three years later another fire swept from
London Bridge to St. Clement Danes, involving St. Paul's. In
1161 London, Canterbury, Winchester, and Exeter were all
devastated by fire. Winchester was burnt again in 1180, Glaston-
bury in 1184, and Chichester in 1187. The only method of
checking a fire when once it had started was by pulling down
houses—and in particular thatched roofs—so as to prevent it
spreading, and special hooks and ropes had to be kept in every
ward, or division, of the town for this purpose. Precautionary
measures began to be adopted after a while, and in London in
1189 a building by-law was issued by which all houses had to be
built partly of stone and roofed with tiles, and this was gradually
adopted in other towns, though at Norwich thatched roofs were
not forbidden until the sixteenth century. Anything in the
nature of an effective fire-brigade was impossible without a high
pressure water supply; the water would have to be drawn from
wells or a river and carried in buckets.

The system of collecting water in reservoirs or from springs
on high ground and distributing it through pipes—of wood,
earthenware, or lead—seems to have begun in the larger monastic
houses, which also had usually underground sewers flushed by
a flowing stream of water. There still exists an elaborate plan
of the waterworks of the cathedral priory of Canterbury, drawn
in the twelfth century, and later plans of those of other houses.
The first 'conduit' or water-main in London was laid down in the
thirteenth century, and brought water from springs at Tyburn
to a fountain in West Cheap; it was only intended to provide
water for the poor to drink, and for the wealthier classes (who did
not drink water, regarding it as the last resource of thirsty
poverty), to cook their food with, and there were regulations
constantly made, and as constantly broken, against its use by
brewers, cooks, and fishmongers. Other conduits were laid down
during the fifteenth and sixteenth centuries, and at the end of the
sixteenth century something in the nature of water-towers
supplied by pumping appears to have been introduced.

No kind of central drainage system was dreamt of in the Middle Ages. Great houses, especially monasteries, had their private system of sanitation, as has been mentioned, when flowing water was available ; for the rest, filth and garbage of all kinds was thrown into the streets and left there until the town officials made a fuss, when it was carted away and dumped into the river or some other convenient place. The streets even in London must have been noisome, and when we find Edward III moved to complain that the smells of York were worse than those of any other town in the kingdom we can believe that that city was no health resort. In such conditions it is not surprising that outbreaks of plague should have been frequent and severe.

The town authorities realized the danger of insanitary conditions and made constant efforts to improve matters, but they were handicapped by the oriental fatalism of the uneducated classes, who, like Turks or Indians, regarded disease as an act of God and would make no effort to avoid it. The first national Sanitation Act, applying to all towns, was passed in 1388 by a parliament sitting at Cambridge, and seems to have been inspired by the peculiarly filthy condition of that royal and learned borough. It consisted of a general prohibition of the pollution of rivers, ditches and open spaces, and did little more than give parliamentary support to the by-laws on that subject which already existed in all the larger towns. Nuisances of a less dangerous kind were also dealt with in by-laws ; unsavoury trades, such as the dressing of skins, tanning, and brick-burning, were usually banished to the outskirts of the town, and attempts were made to prevent the use of pit coal instead of charcoal for burning lime, on the ground that the fumes were unpleasant. It is, indeed, interesting to notice that the pollution of the air with the smoke of pit coal, an urgent problem of the present day, was already a subject of complaint some six hundred and fifty years ago, when Queen Eleanor of Provence, the pious but asthmatic wife of Henry III, was driven away from Nottingham by the poisonous fumes of coal fires.

IV

HOME LIFE

In dealing with the dwellings of our ancestors the threefold division of society becomes evident ; we have to consider the cottages of the labourers, the houses of the middle class, and the castles or palaces of the nobles. The cottages need not detain us long ; in construction they represent the least that men must have to protect them from wet and cold—four walls and a roof. The walls were of mud or of ' wattle-and-daub ', that is to say a framework of upright stakes interwoven with osiers or other pliable strips of wood in the manner of a wattled hurdle, coated with clay rammed well into the spaces between the wattles. In one wall a space would be left for entrance, which might or might not be fitted with a door, and there would usually be one or two small openings, windows, to admit light. A roof of thatch and a floor of trodden earth complete the picture. Within this single room, blackened by smoke from the wood fire lit in the middle of the floor in winter or when the weather was too wet to do their cooking outside, lived the cottager's family : their furniture a table and a few rough stools, a chest, an iron cauldron and a few bowls, mugs and pitchers of earthenware : their beds heaps of straw or bracken covered with coarse woollen rugs. Yet we need not waste much pity on them ; one's idea of comfort or discomfort is determined mainly by what one is used to, and partly by how much worse or better off one's neighbours are. ' The curse of sorrow is comparison '—and comparison especially with what the sufferer might reasonably expect. The lot of a working-man of the present day who has to bring up his family in a single room of a dreary tenement-building or in a squalid hovel in some mining village is embittered by the knowledge that other men of his own class have comparatively luxurious homes ; but the medieval peasant was little worse off than the small farmer for whom he worked, and often not very far removed from the lord of the manor himself. William Harrison, writing in the reign of Elizabeth, after the Middle Ages were over, says that old men in his village talked of

' the great amendment of lodging ; for, said they, our fathers, yea and we ourselves also, have lain full oft upon straw pallets, on rough mats covered only with a sheet, under coverlets made of dagswain or hopharlots (I use their own terms), and a good

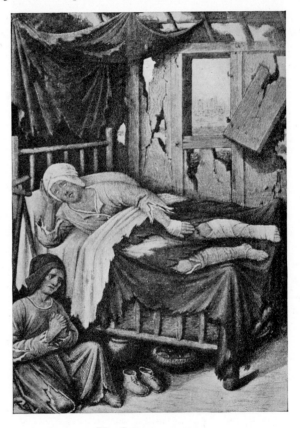

The Cottager : c. 1500.

round log under their heads instead of a bolster or pillow. If it were so that our fathers—or the good man of the house—had within seven years after his marriage purchased a mattress or flock bed, and thereto a stack of chaff to rest his head upon, he thought himself to be as well lodged as the lord of the town, that peradventure lay seldom in a bed of down or whole feathers, so well were they content, and with such base kind of furniture : which also is not very much amended as yet in some parts of Bedfordshire and elsewhere further off from our southern parts. Pillows (said they) were thought meet only for women in child-bed. As for servants, if they had any sheet above them, it was well, for seldom had they any under their bodies to keep them from the pricking straws that ran oft through the canvas of the pallet and rased their hardened hides.'

At the opposite end of the social scale were the dwellings of the great nobles. The Norman noble, being by training a man of war and by virtue of the Conquest a detested alien, naturally thought of safety first and built for his residence a castle. In almost every town of any size such a castle was constructed, not for the protection of the town, but in order to overawe the towns-folk. Even when the Norman rule had become an accepted fact and rebellions were no longer to be feared, the building of castles went on, but now for the protection of the owner against the violence of rival lords. With the military features of these castles we shall deal elsewhere. Considered as dwellings most of them would not have appealed to later, more luxurious ages. A typical castle consisted of two parts ; a courtyard, surrounded by a ditch and wall, and a keep, a massive tower, usually standing on an artificial mound at one end of the courtyard. In the earlier and smaller examples the living-rooms were in the keep, but when the outer defences of the court were strong it was found more convenient to place them in the court, either built up against the outer wall or grouped as a separate house standing within the protected area. In any case the chief room would be the great hall, where the lord of the castle and all his household and retainers took their meals and spent their spare time, and where many of the household slept. This hall was often, as for instance at Oakham or Winchester, where such halls still stand, a very large building, divided lengthwise by rows of pillars and much resembling the nave of a church, except that if one of its walls formed part of the defences of the castle, the windows on

The Craftsman: c. 1500

The Noble: c. 1500

that side would be narrow slits. At one end of the hall would be the kitchen, and elsewhere the chapel and bedrooms, of which the positions would be determined by the military needs of the building. As time went on luxury and wealth increased and the power of the central government restricted private warfare ; the castles gradually lost their military character and became merely fortified houses, strong enough to resist a casual raid but not built to withstand a siege, and so develop into the great Tudor houses, such as Hampton Court.

In the medieval house, even more than in the castle, the main feature was the hall. This was a room, usually from one and a half to twice as long as it was broad, open to the full height of the house. Across one end of the room, often on a raised dais, was the high table, where sat the master of the house, his family and guests ; while at right angles to this, running lengthwise down the hall, were the tables for the servants. On a stone hearth in the middle of the floor was the fire, the smoke from which found its way out through a ' louvre ' (a hole in the roof covered by a little turret with open sides), leaving a black deposit of soot on the roof beams, and, if the house were that of a farmer, on the flitches of bacon and sides of salted beef hanging in the roof. Originally the food was cooked as well as eaten in the hall, and it was probably partly to avoid the noise, smell, and heat of the cooking operations that a wooden partition or screen was built across the lower end of the hall. Such a screen, with two doors in it, became a permanent feature in the medieval hall, even when regular kitchen offices were built beyond the lower end of the hall ; in the larger houses it usually carried a gallery, where musicians would play during meals. Into the passage behind the screen opened, in the side wall, the door from outside (often covered by a porch), and, in the end wall, three doors, that in the centre leading to the kitchen, those on either side to the buttery, where the wine and ale were kept, and the pantry or bread store. Such was the typical arrangement of the lower end of the hall in a large house, as may be seen in most of the colleges at Oxford or Cambridge, an arrangement which might be slightly modified in small houses. At the upper or high table end of the hall a door led into the 'chamber' or sleeping-room of the family, which also served in the daytime as the 'bower' or special apartment of the ladies. After the twelfth century it became usual to divide this building at the upper end of the hall into two stories, the lower being used as a withdrawing-room or parlour and the upper—the 'solar' ('the sunny room', from

Oakham Castle Hall.

Latin *sol*)—reached by an outside staircase, as bedroom. These rooms were furnished with fireplaces built into the wall, with chimneys, and when, in the sixteenth century, at the very end of the medieval period, similar wall fireplaces began to take the place of the central hearth in the hall, the necessity for having the hall open to the roof ceased; consequently we find that from Tudor times onwards a decreasing number of houses were built with open halls, and more and more of such existing halls were divided into two or three stories, so that often the original plan of the house is quite lost, and it is only by climbing up into the roof and finding the rafters blackened by the smoke of the former central fire that we can be sure that the house is medieval.

In the houses of the nobles the windows might be filled with stained glass, but in ordinary houses they would be unglazed, and until the sixteenth century glass was considered a luxury. Sometimes the window opening would be filled with a lattice of wood or metal, occasionally oiled linen would be stretched across it, but most often it would be open to the wind and rain, which could, however, be excluded by closing the oak shutters with which the windows were provided. The walls were plastered and painted with bright colours, sometimes with scenes from biblical history, romances, legends of the saints or allegorical subjects such as the Wheel of Fortune or the representation of Winter ' with a sad and miserable face ', which Henry III ordered to be painted over the fireplace in one of his rooms. With the increase of wealth in the fifteenth century it became the fashion to hang the walls with gorgeous tapestries and eastern embroideries. Even in earlier times it was usual to hang a strip of bright material behind the benches in the hall, with a panel of some richer stuff, often carried up to form a canopy, for the seats of the master and mistress of the house at the centre of the high table.

The tables, which were for the most part movable constructions of boards on trestles, were always covered with linen cloths. On these were set out spoons, knives—forks were a curiosity in England even as late as the time of Elizabeth—cups and jugs of wood and earthenware. Among the wealthy it was the custom to make a great display of gold and silver vessels—cups and salt cellars and purely ornamental pieces, such as the ' nef ', an elaborate piece of plate in the shape of a ship ; such plate as could not be placed upon the table was exhibited on the shelves of the cupboard (a name afterwards transferred to the receptacle in which the plate was locked up). During the prosperous days of the fifteenth century, also, pewter—an alloy of tin and lead for which England was famous—largely supplanted the wooden platters of earlier times. Earthenware does not seem to have been used for plates, and indeed very often meat was eaten on trenchers, or thick slices of bread, which were afterwards given to the poor or, with the bones off which the diners had gnawed most of the meat, flung on to the floor for the dogs. As the floor was covered with straw or rushes, none too frequently changed, the unsavoury and smelly state of the hall may well be imagined—it was, indeed, one of the features of English home life which impressed Erasmus most unfavourably. A great improvement in table manners was effected by the introduction of carpets, but that only occurred in comparatively recent times, carpets being regarded throughout the Middle Ages as a foreign fashion and the extreme height of luxury.

Andrew Borde, a shrewd physician in the time of Henry VIII, wrote : ' Two meales a daye is suffycyent for a rest man ; and a laborer may eate three tymes a day ; and he that doth eate ofter lyveth a beestly lyfe.' The two universal meals were dinner, taken about 10 or 11 in the morning, and supper, for which the usual hour was 4 o'clock ; breakfast as a regular meal is little heard of, though probably most men started the day with a draught of ale and some bread, but the more luxurious indulged in ' rere-suppers ' at night, which were often denounced as an occasion of drunkenness. Dinner and supper were substantial meals, which naturally varied very much according to the wealth of the householder. The English peasant, unlike those of the same class on the Continent, had meat—bacon, beef, or at least a herring—almost every day, as well as bread and cheese ; the ordinary gentleman dining by himself would have two or three dishes of meat and sweets ; the nobleman, who was bound by tradition to keep open house and show hospitality to all comers, would have a dinner of two or three courses, each course consisting of a score of different dishes, meat, fish, game, and sweets mingled indiscriminately, ending with fruit and nuts. In a great house the serving of the dinner, from the laying of the table-cloth to its removal, was a ceremony conducted with the solemn precision of a religious rite, and a knowledge of the correct method of carving the innumerable kinds of meat was part of the necessary education of a gentleman. In less polite society, when the meat was put on the table for the diners to help themselves, there were not infrequently unseemly scrambles and such points of good manners as washing the hands before meals, not putting more than a thumb and two fingers on the joint when carving it and not picking the teeth with a knife were apt to be disregarded.

While solid meats, such as beef and mutton and the famous boar's head associated with Christmas feasts, figured to some extent at most dinners, medieval cookery was much more elaborate than is often realized. A great variety of soups, stews, pasties, fritters, jellies, and so forth, were in common use, and the recipes that have survived from the fifteenth century show that many dishes were of very elaborate composition, most containing quantities of spices. As a single instance we may take the recipe for 'leche lumbard', a very favourite dish, something in the nature of a saveloy or German sausage : Take pork and pound it in a mortar with eggs ; add sugar, salt, raisins, currants, minced dates, powdered pepper and cloves ; put it in a bladder and boil it ; then cut it in slices. This was served with a sauce made of raisins, red wine, almond-milk coloured with saffron, pepper, cloves, cinnamon and ginger. Fish also played a very important part in the medieval kitchen, especially as during Lent and on fast days, which included all Fridays, no flesh might be eaten. The herring was the fish in greatest demand, either fresh, salted, or smoked, but every known fish from the minnow to the whale figured on the medieval bill of fare. Of fruits several varieties of pears (of which 'Wardens' were famed for their excellence in pies) and apples were grown in the country, as were cherries, damsons, and plums ; pomegranates and oranges, imported from Spain, were luxuries for the rich, but strawberries (of the little, wild kind) and cream formed a combination as much appreciated by all classes in the Middle Ages as at the present day. Strawberries, barberries, and other fruits were also made into ' comfits ' or sweets and ' conserve ' or jam, while

A Humble Meal: 1415

A Rich Banquet: c. 1416

The walls are hung with tapestry representing a battle scene; over the master of the house is a canopy and behind him a wicker fire-screen. The carver has a towel over his shoulder; above him is the steward with his rod of office

G

'marmelade', originally made of quinces, was another Spanish
luxury. Many kinds of wine, from France, Spain, Italy, and the
Levant, were in use, but the common drink of all classes was ale,
of which prodigious quantities were consumed. Every household
of any size brewed its own ale, and ale was coupled with bread
as one of the two commodities of which the quality and price
had to be controlled by the local authorities. During the fifteenth
century the Dutch, of whom there were a great many in London
and the eastern counties, introduced beer—a form of malt liquor
like ale, but made bitter with hops. At first the new drink was
denounced as poison, but it rapidly became popular and by the
end of the medieval period beer was supplanting ale as the
universal drink.

During dinner, which was a lengthy as well as a heavy meal,
there would often be music, either from a band of musicians in
the gallery at the lower end of the hall or from some wandering
minstrel or harper, who would sing old ballads of Robin Hood
or Sir Lancelot, and the latest topical song in mockery of some
unpopular minister, or would improvise a song in praise of the
master of the house and his guests. When the tables had been
cleared the ladies would retire to their chamber while the men
remained drinking. Then, if the weather were fine, there would
be dancing outside upon the grass, the English being especially
famed for their 'caroles' in which song and dance were combined. More elaborate than these simple, graceful country dances
were the morris dances, supposed to have been invented by the
Moorish inhabitants of Southern Spain, in which the dancers
wearing costumes covered with little bells and carrying staves in
their hands, executed complicated figures. These morris dances
were particularly associated with the gaieties of Christmas and
the New Year, as were also the 'mummings', in which those who
took part wore masks and quaint costumes and performed plays
or grotesque ballets. The love of dressing-up, which all children
and the wiser of their elders always have, was strong in medieval
days, and kings and their nobles often indulged in the practice when
an excuse presented itself. Such an occasion was the season of

Christmas, when the hall was a scene of gaiety—feasting, dancing, mumming and all kinds of games. Among these games two of the most popular were ' hot cockles ', in which one player knelt down, blindfolded, and was struck—none too gently—by other players, whose identity he had to guess, and ' hoodman blind ' (the modern ' blind man's buff '), in which one player had his face covered by reversing his hood and had to catch the others. At the head of all the riotous fun was ' the lord of misrule ', one of the servants, who wore a fantastic costume and held absolute

Dancing: c. 1300.

sway as King of Christmas, whose orders even the master of the house must obey, though if he was wise he did not take too great liberties, remembering that Christmas comes but once a year and that when his brief reign was over he would be again a servant very much at the mercy of his master.

After dinner in the summer the ladies would walk in the garden, gathering flowers, and weaving them into garlands, for our ancestors were fond of flowers and a garden was attached to every great house. In it would be grown roses, lilies, gilliflowers (clove-pinks), marigolds, periwinkle, sweet and aromatic plants, used for perfuming the rooms, such as lavender, rosemary and juniper, and an abundance of herbs for use in cookery or medicine.

Meals were not infrequently taken in the garden, and even picnics were not unknown, though usually they were held less for the pleasure of eating out of doors than because a hunting expedition made any other kind of meal impossible. Hunting and hawking were chief sports of the gentry, but, contrary to present ideas, the fox was not considered worth hunting, it was looked upon as vermin and classed with wild cats and wolves (which were still not uncommon in England at the beginning of the thirteenth century), as an animal to be pursued for its destruction rather than for sport. The beasts of chase were deer and wild boars and hares, and these were preserved under very strict game laws. Ladies took part in hunting the deer and hares and also in hawking. The quarry in the latter case would be waterfowl—ducks, cranes, and herons—and several varieties of hawks and falcons were used, really good birds being exceedingly valuable. Falcons often figure among the presents sent by kings to those whom they wished to honour, and pilgrimages were made to the shrines of saints for the recovery of sick hawks. Packs of hounds were also kept for sporting purposes; spaniels to put up birds for the hawks, greyhounds for the pursuit of hares and deer, and nondescript dogs of the mastiff type for hunting the formidable boar. Judging from pictures, there must have been almost as many varieties of dogs in the fifteenth as there are in the twentieth century, ranging from the great savage watch-dogs down to the little lap-dogs of which ladies so often made pets. The favourite lap-dogs were Maltese spaniels:

'These are little and prettie, proper and fine, and sought out far and neere to satisfy the nice delicacie of daintie dames and wanton women's willes; instruments of follie to play and dallie withal, in trifling away the treasure of time, to withdraw their minds from more commendable exercises, a sillie poore shift to shun their irkesome idleness. These puppies, the smaller they be the better they are accepted, the more pleasure also they provoke, as meet plaiefellows for minsing mistresses to beare in their bosoms, to succour with sleep in bed and nourish with meat at board, to lie in their laps and licke their lips as they lie in their wagons and coches. . . . Some of this kind of people delight mor

in their dogs, that are deprived of all possibilitie of reason, than
they do in children that are capable of wisedome and judgement.
Yea, they oft feed them of the best, where the poore mans child
at their doores can hardlie come by the worst.'

A Garden : c. 1490.

Lap-dogs were not the only pets that women kept, if we may judge
from the fact that in 1387 the Bishop of Winchester had to rebuke
certain nuns for bringing to church with them ' birds, rabbits,
hounds, and such like frivolous things, whereunto they give more
heed than to the offices of the church '. Caged birds were

certainly quite common in the medieval house; larks and nightin-
gales were kept for their song, magpies and 'popinjays' (parrots
—brought from the East originally by the Crusaders) for their
power of talking; squirrels were sometimes kept, as were also
monkeys, but cats, though they were employed to catch mice,
do not seem to have been regarded as pets as a rule.

Returning to the hall from the garden, the hunt or more
arduous employments, the household would partake of a supper
very similar to their previous dinner. The meal might be slightly
less solid, but it was usually even more prolonged, especially in
the matter of drinking. When the days were short artificial
light would be required, for, as a medieval writer observes, 'it is
shame to suppe in darknes, and perillous also for flyes and other
filth'; such light they would obtain mainly from candles, the
poorer sort made of tallow, the better of purified beeswax.
Lamps, consisting of a cotton wick floating in a bowl of vegetable
or fish oil, were more valuable for their remaining alight for a long
time than for their illumination, which was feeble, and torches
of resinous wood, though bright, must have been a source of much
smoke and no little danger. Early hours were the rule; even in
Shakespeare's time to have 'heard the chimes at midnight'
was a sign of singular dissipation, while in medieval days to be
still in bed after six o'clock in the morning was the mark of
a sluggard; so, except in the height of summer, most of the
company would retire to their beds soon after supper was over.
If there was time to be passed before retiring, it would probably
be spent either in the hall or in the withdrawing-room playing
games of skill, usually for money. Of these games chess was the
most ancient and famous. Chess certainly originated in the East,
but it had been introduced into Europe before the end of the
eleventh century and spread all over the Continent. Stories of
fatal quarrels over chess are common in medieval romances, and
elaborately carved ivory chessmen of the twelfth and thirteenth
centuries may be seen in museums, while Edward I is known to
have received a present of a set of chessmen of jasper and crystal.
Almost equal to chess in popularity was 'tables', which was

Supper by Candlelight : 14th century

A Game of Chess : c. 1500

practically a form of our backgammon, being played with dice and draughtsmen; references to this game are very numerous, and it was apparently sometimes played with partners, as King John is found on various occasions 'playing at tables' in partnership with nobles such as Payn de Chaworth or Brian de Lisle and with a wealthy London merchant, John Bucquinte. Draughts, then known as 'ladies', was less popular, but gambling with dice was extremely common and carried to great lengths, whole estates being staked on a single throw. Playing-cards, which are said, like chess, to have originated in the East, were certainly known in Europe by the middle of the fourteenth century, but there is not much evidence of their use in England until about a hundred years later; by the time of Edward IV, however, they were well established here and rapidly increased in popularity, but of the exact nature of medieval card games very little appears to be known.

Medieval ideas of propriety were different from ours, and it was usual for all the members of a family, including their guests, to sleep in one chamber—it would indeed have been difficult for them to do otherwise when the ordinary house only contained one sleeping apartment. This seems all the more repugnant to our ideas as everybody slept naked, night-clothes being practically unknown before the sixteenth century. The bedsteads in Norman times were low, couch-like frames of wood; as time went on these frames became higher and more elaborate, the head of the bed was carried up, as a panel, either of carved wood or more often of embroidered stuff, and known as the 'tester' (from the old French *teste* = a head); from the top of the 'tester' a canopy or 'seler' stretched over the bed and from each corner of this canopy hung curtains, which were kept looped up in the daytime but could be pulled so as to enclose the whole bed. The final development was the well-known 'four-post bed' of Tudor and later times. A low 'truckle bed' was often kept under the great bed and brought out at night for the use of a servant or other inferior. The ordinary mattress was stuffed with straw, but the more luxurious slept upon feather-beds. Linen sheets were in use from very early times, but not, as we have already seen, for servants ; blankets and rugs were plentiful, and over all would be a coverlid, quilted or embroidered, or, in winter, made of fur. The embroideries were often of great beauty and ' a bed ', by which was meant a complete set of hangings, was a common bequest in medieval wills, and by no means to be despised, seeing that such beds in the fifteenth century were not infrequently valued at from fifty to a hundred pounds.

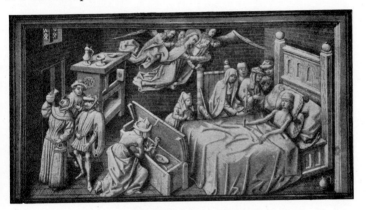

A Bedchamber : c. 1460.
The Blessed Virgin appearing in a vision to a dying man.

The walls of the chamber might be panelled in wood, but more often they would be hung with tapestry or painted canvas. For furniture there would be at least one chair by the bedside and a chest ; there might be other chairs or stools, but the bed itself was used as a seat in the daytime. An English writer of the twelfth century says that there should also be two rods projecting from the wall, one as a perch for the hawk and the other to hang clothes upon. The latter was certainly usual, but it seems doubtful if many persons carried their fondness for their hawks to the point of keeping them in their bedrooms—it was probably considered healthier for the hawks that they should have a place to themselves.

In the better-class bedrooms there would usually be a wash-stand, or rather a cupboard on which stood a metal basin and jug. Medieval books of etiquette insist upon the duty of washing hands, face, and teeth every morning, but say nothing on the subject of an occasional bath. An early English writer refers to the Danes' habit of taking a bath on Saturdays as an instance of their foppishness, and the monks went even further in laying down the rule that a bath should only be taken for reasons of health when ordered by the doctor. The detailed accounts of King John's household show that that monarch indulged in a bath about once in three weeks. On the other hand, we read in innumerable romances that it was the first act of hospitality, on the arrival of a visitor at a castle, to provide him with a bath, and the illustrations to these romances show that great houses often had a kind of bath-room, a curtained alcove containing a large tub. Whether soap was used for personal washing is not certain, but it, and a lye made from wood ashes, was used for washing clothes. In which connexion it is rather interesting to notice that laundresses were in the habit of losing things and sending back the wrong clothes even in the reign of Edward VI, as in an inventory of the Earl of Warwick's wardrobe in 1550 mention is made of two shirts which ' were lost at the landry at Ely House ' and of another which was ' changed at wasshyng '.

Although, as we have seen, the ordinary house during the greater part of the Middle Ages had only one sleeping chamber, this was not the case with the palaces of kings and nobles ; yet even there the number of rooms for guests was limited and the accommodation for the household was far from luxurious. The lower servants, when they did not sleep in the hall, slept in the kitchen, outhouses, or wherever they could find a place ; those of higher rank probably shared a common dormitory and certainly shared beds. Even in the household of the great Percy family, Earls of Northumberland, as late as the beginning of the sixteenth century the chaplains slept two to a bed, and the children, or choir-boys, three in one bed. In fact in considering home life

n the Middle Ages one is struck by the curious combination of
luxury and discomfort, and by the lack of privacy. Though the
man of rank had legal privileges against the poor man which

A Bath: c. 1415.

would be considered intolerable now, the two were in closer
touch than they are at the present time. The process of drawing
apart began with the increase of wealth at the end of the fourteenth century, when the author of *Piers Plowman*, writing
shortly before the Peasants' Rising of 1381, comments on the

growing custom of gentlemen dining apart from their household in their private rooms.

> Wretched is the hall where lord and lady will not sit.
> Now have the rich a rule to eat by themselves,
> In a private parlour or in a chamber with a chimney
> Because of the poor in the hall.

The change in the design of houses when the great hall disappeared and rooms become more numerous, making it easier to separate the servants from the family, favoured the process, as did the rise of a ' new rich ' class, without the old traditions, in Tudor times; and it ended by producing a race who keep themselves to themselves and boast that ' an Englishman's house is his castle '.

V

THE CHURCH AND RELIGION

THE medieval period might be called the Age of Faith and the modern the Age of Faiths. In the Middle Ages there was for all Western Europe only one form of religion—that taught by the Catholic Church, of which the acknowledged head was the Pope of Rome. No man might think for himself in matters of religion or hold any views different from those laid down by the Church ; if he did he was a heretic and acted at the peril of his body in this world and his soul in the next. The Reformation being by nature a Protestant movement, it was natural that various groups of reformers should protest with varying vigour against particular beliefs and practices of the Roman Church, and should go on to protest equally strongly against each other's attitude ; so that while the Roman Church continued united and unalterable, the Reformed Church rapidly split up into innumerable sects, which have gone on multiplying down to the present day.

England throughout the Middle Ages was definitely part of the Catholic Roman Church ; but the English did not accept the interference of the Pope in their affairs quite so readily as did the continental nations. William the Conqueror had definitely refused to admit the Pope's claim to be his over-lord ; Henry II, in his struggle to make the Church submit to the State in matters of law, had the support of a large part of the nation, until the murder of Becket put him hopelessly in the wrong ; King John's action in acknowledging the Pope as over-lord of England, though recognized as a clever stroke of policy, roused a good deal of resentment ; under Henry III the English clergy spoke their mind very freely on the subject of papal interference and taxation, while in the next reign, when the Pope claimed to dispose of the Scottish throne, the Barons told him bluntly to mind his own business ; from the time of Edward III the English, clergy as well as laity, grew more and more impatient of papal control. But this did not affect their belief, and until the middle of the fourteenth century no one in this country doubted the truth of the religion of their ancestors—except such evil-livers as scoffed at all religion—or the position of the Pope as head of the Church. Then, in 1349, came the terrible Black Death, which had two opposite effects upon the minds of men ; some became reckless and abandoned themselves to every kind of wickedness, but many turned more seriously to thoughts of religion. The Church at that time had become very worldly and corrupt, and the papal court in particular was notorious for greed and immorality ; added to which, there was a ' schism ' or split in the Church, so that there were actually rival popes, each claiming to be the head of the Church. When John Wycliffe, of whom some account will be given in a later chapter, attacked the corruption of the Church, he at once received the support of a large number of earnest men—but not of the Pope or bishops. When he went on to attack the doctrines of the Church, particularly ' transubstantiation '—the belief in the conversion of the bread and wine, when consecrated in the service of the Mass, into the actual body and blood of Christ—and the worship of saints and relics, he and his followers (who went further than he) again found willing hearers, and during the first half of the fifteenth century England was full of the heresy of the Lollards. But the time for a Protestant reformation had not yet come ; the powers of the Church and the State were united to crush out heresy, and the English people continued to hold the Catholic faith and to look to Rome for guidance, until Henry VIII, for purely personal reasons, severed the English Church from the control of the Pope (whereat many rejoiced) and, more or less accidentally, let loose the flood of reforming Protestantism (whereat a few exulted).

One of the doctrines of the Lollards was the equality of all men, and this was also upheld by the Church, in theory and to a large extent in practice. The Church was in theory a completely democratic body. The son of a peasant, if he became

Mass : 15th century

The Elevation of the Host

a priest, might rise to be a bishop or even, as Pope, become the superior of all the kings of Europe. The only Englishman who ever became Pope—Nicholas Brakespere (Pope Adrian IV)—was the son of a humble townsman of St. Albans, and Cardinal Wolsey was the son of a small farmer. Even villeins, when once they had obtained leave from their lords to take holy orders, had a chance of rising to these heights. In theory also, the Church looked upon all laymen, rich and poor alike as equal, and punished the sins of all alike, but the actual practice of the Church courts is shown in their proceedings in Kent in 1292, when severe penances were put upon persons of humble position, but Sir Thomas de Marynes was allowed to pay a fine, as 'it was not seemly for a knight to do public penance'. Still, the Church could stand up against the nobles and did form a certain restraint upon their power over the poor. And however far the Church as a whole fell short of Christian ideals, there were always many good priests to teach those ideals, by word and example, and to uphold truth and justice.

Another point in which practice fell far short of theory was in the religious education of the people. Every person was supposed to know at least the Paternoster (Lord's Prayer), Creed, and *Ave Maria* (or Angelic Salutation), either in Latin or in English. Yet many grew up without even so much knowledge of their services, and many more knew nothing about the meaning of the Latin services which they heard in their churches. Nor was this surprising, when often the priests themselves were little wiser than their parishioners. All through the Middle Ages we find continual complaints of the appalling ignorance of many of the clergy. ' Parson Sloth,' in the *Vision of Piers Plowman*, confesses :

I have been priest and parson for thirty winters past,
But I cannot solfa or sing, or read a Latin life of saints ;
But I can find a hare, in a field or in a furrow,
Better than construe the first Psalm or explain it to the parish.
I can hold a friendly meeting, I can cast a shire's accounts,
But in mass-book or Pope's edict I cannot read a line.

his might be thought a poetic exaggeration, but a visitation of eventeen parishes in Berkshire in 1222 showed that five of the lergy could neither construe nor sing the Mass, and other records how that such a state of affairs was not uncommon. Bishop Hooper's visitation in 1552 is said to have shown ' scores of lergy who could not tell who was the author of the Lord's Prayer, or where it was to be found '. When Louis de Beaumont became Bishop of Durham in 1316, it is said that ' he understood not Latin, and could scarce pronounce it. When, therefore, at his consecration, he should have made his formal profession, he could not read it, though he had been instructed therein for many days beforehand ; and having at last arrived, with many promptings from others, at the word *Metropolitan*, which after many gasps he yet could not pronounce, at length he said in the French tongue, " Let that be taken as read ! " All the bystanders were amazed, mourning that such a man should be consecrated bishop. Another time, when he was conferring Holy Orders, and could not pronounce that phrase *in aenigmate*, he said in French to those that stood by, " By St. Louis, the man was a clown that wrote this word ! " '

The use of Latin as the universal language of the Church had his advantage, that a man who knew the service could join in it wherever he might be—an Englishman would be as much at home in a German, French, and Italian church as in the church of his own parish. But it had the obvious disadvantage that if he did not know Latin and had not been properly instructed he would be as little at home in his parish church as he would be in a foreign land. A great preacher of the thirteenth century pictures his congregation saying, ' We understand not the Mass, and cannot pray thereat so well as we should, nor feel so great reverence as if we understood it. We understand every word of the sermon, but the Mass we understand not, nor know what is being read or sung ; we cannot comprehend it.' Such ignorance of priests and people led to much slovenliness on the part of the clergy and irreverence on the part of the congregation, who laughed and chattered during the services, hardly troubling to

doff their caps and kneel at the supreme moment of the Mass
—the consecration of the elements—which was announced b
the ringing of the Sanctus bell. St. Bernardino said :

' There are many ignorant folk who, when the priest is cele
brating, come drunken from the taverns or wait outside th
church, talking of their oxen and worldly matters, and even
obscenities ; nor do they enter the church until the elevation
at which they gaze in utter irreverence, with their heads partl
or wholly covered and their stiff knees scarcely bowed ; and thu
—after running noisily to see the Body of Christ, half inside an
half outside the church—suddenly, after the barest glimpse
Him, they run off again as hastily as if they had seen not Chris
but the Devil ! '

Yet where a parish was fortunate enough to have such a parso
as Chaucer pictures for us, we may be sure that all were taugh
to know and understand and love their services.   There th
majority would start the day by attending early Mass at si
o'clock.   On Sundays and festivals they would also come to th
High Mass at 9 or 10, in the course of which there would b
a sermon in English.   The nature of the sermon would depend
as it still does, upon the nature of the preacher ; the lazy coul
buy volumes of sermons ready-made, the conscientious migh
deliver learned discourses, but often the sermon was more
a personal talk, enlivened with stories, frequently humorous
fables, or comparisons drawn from popular books of natura
history.   It was from the pulpit that the people received thei
religious instruction, and although preaching never in pre
Reformation days held such a place in the services as it did i
Puritan times, it did play a very important part.

Sunday was a day set apart for worship, and all work wa
forbidden, except what was really necessary, such as the cookin
of food or the shoeing of a traveller's horse or the carrying of th
harvest.   Buying and selling were also forbidden, but in spit
of constant prohibitions, markets continued to be held o
Sundays in some places, and similarly the Courts of Law some
times sat on Sunday.   The greater Saints' days were also day
on which no work might be done, and in particular the day

A Bishop preaching

A Friar preaching outside a Church : c. 1480

the saint to whom the parish church was dedicated; but in this case the fact that all the people of the parish would be collected, in holiday mood, in the neighbourhood of the church for a special service, led to the erection of stalls, first of all to supply them with food and drink and then for the sale of less necessary articles, thus developing into a regular fair. So much was this the case that where, as has often happened in the centuries since the Reformation, the dedication of a church has been forgotten, it is often possible to recover it by finding the date of the village fair and seeing what saint was commemorated on that day.

The centre of religious life was naturally the parish church. Usually this was built in the first place by the lord of the manor, who therefore had the right of presenting the priest to serve it. This priest was called the rector (=ruler) or parson (=the chief person) of the parish; he was given a house, a certain amount of land (called the glebe), and a yearly sum of money, chiefly derived from tithes. From a very early period it had been the custom for all Christians to set apart a tenth part of their goods —their crops, cattle, or the profits of their trading—for the service of God. When the country came to be divided up into parishes these tenths, or tithes, were naturally assigned to the church of the parish. Out of this sum the rector had to keep the church in repair, assist the poor, and show hospitality to visitors. Some rectors could hardly live on the money they received, but many churches were worth large sums; the rectors of these wealthy churches usually took the greater part of the money and sent a vicar (=a substitute) to do all the work of the parish for a small sum. The lord of a manor would often give the advowson of his church, that is to say the right of presenting a rector, to a monastery; then, if the living was wealthy, the monks would get leave from the bishop to ' appropriate ' the church, by which they became rectors and could appoint a vicar to serve the parish. Usually in these cases the rector kept the ' great tithes ' of corn and wool, and the vicar had the ' lesser tithes ' of practically everything else, from cabbages to coal-mines.

Every church consisted of at least two parts : a chancel, at the east end,[1] in which was the high altar (the communion-table of Protestant churches), and a nave to the west. The chancel was the priest's portion and had to be repaired by the rector ; the nave was used by the parishioners and they were responsible for its up-keep. Thus when Bodmin church was rebuilt in the

Peasants paying Tithes in kind : one leading a lamb, another carrying a goose : 1479.

fifteenth century, practically everybody in the parish seems to have contributed to the expense, and when a new tower was built at Totnes, all the townsmen were called upon to help in bringing the stone from the quarry to the church. There is plenty of evidence that the people were proud of their churches, and gave liberally to make them beautiful. It is to this parochial patriotism that we owe the splendid churches of East Anglia

[1] Churches were built to lie east and west when possible, but in towns their position depended on the space available and they might even lie north and south.

and the West country, built in the fifteenth century when those districts were the centres of the flourishing cloth industry. Nor were they content to have splendid buildings, but every church was rich in ornaments—embroidered vestments for the priests, altar hangings, banners and crosses, chalices and images. The wealth of even insignificant parish churches before the Reformation is surprising, while if the treasures of one of the greater churches had survived to the present time they would be worth a king's ransom.

In most churches the chancel was structurally separated from the nave by the chancel-arch ; but in any case there was across the dividing line a wooden screen carrying a gallery, known as the rood-loft, because upon it stood the rood or crucifix ; from this gallery the priest was supposed to read the Epistle and Gospel, but this was only done in the greater churches. The roods and most of the rood-lofts have been destroyed, but numbers of screens, some beautifully carved and painted, still exist ; and even where the screens have disappeared, the steps and doorway leading to the loft can often be seen in the wall beside the chancel-arch.

Besides the high altar at the East end of the chancel, there would be a number of other altars in the nave and side chapels in honour of various saints, and in most churches some of these would be associated with gilds. These gilds, which were something like our ' friendly societies ', were associations of men and women for religious and social purposes. They were always connected with a particular altar or image in the parish church, before which they kept a lamp burning ; often they maintained a chaplain to say Mass at that altar for the souls of members of the gild, in which case the chaplain would also, as a rule, assist the parish priest ; but the main purpose of the gilds was to assist members who fell into poverty or ill health, and to honour their funerals when they died. Such gilds existed in great numbers throughout medieval England, as many as twenty or thirty being sometimes found in a single parish, and did much for the prevention and relief of poverty.

Looking at the church from the outside, the feature most likely to catch one's attention would be the tower, built principally to hold bells. Even where there was no tall tower with a peal of bells there would be at least a little wooden turret with a single bell to summon the people to service. Nor was this the

Baptism : c. 1450.

only purpose that the medieval bell was expected to perform ; for according to the superstition of those days, bells which had duly been christened and blessed by a bishop, by their ringing drove away devils and thunderstorms. On the south side of the nave would be a projecting porch, which played an important part in the lives of the parishioners, as it was at the church porch that the chief part of the marriage service took place.

Inside the church, at the west end, would be the font. Believing as they did that the souls of infants who died unbaptized would be cast into hell, it was natural that our ancestors should administer the sacrament of baptism at the earliest possible opportunity, and it was therefore the custom for a child to be baptized on the day after its birth. Confirmation, it may be observed, followed at a very much earlier age than is now usual in the Church of England; children were expected to be confirmed by the time they were three years old; but although confirmation was a necessary qualification for receiving the sacrament of the Eucharist (or Communion), it is probable that children below the age of twelve did not receive. All above that age were bound to communicate once a year, at Easter, and were expected to do so more frequently. They were also bound to make their Confession at least once a year, at the beginning of Lent, at which season the priest, or priests if there were more than one, sat in the nave of the church to hear the confessions of the penitents, who came and knelt before them.

Mixed with the religion of our ancestors was much superstition. Nor, indeed, is it ever easy to draw a definite line between religion and superstition; beliefs and practices that seem to one person true and helpful will appear to another merely superstitious humbug, but to proclaim them such without regard to the feelings of those that believe in them is no real proof of the disbeliever's superiority in Christianity or manners. Undoubtedly superstitious was the use of sacred objects for magical purposes. Something has already been said about the prevalence of magic and witchcraft; those who practised these wicked arts had a great belief in the power of the Host, or wafer consecrated at the service of the Mass, to protect them from the evil spirits that they tried to call up, and there were cases of such wafers being stolen or bought from unworthy priests. Many who would not go so far as this, would steal water from the font in the belief that it had all kinds of virtues; and so common was this offence that every font had to be supplied with a locked cover. 'Many of the village folk', says Berthold of Ratisbon

in the thirteenth century, ' would come to heaven, were it not
for their witchcrafts. The woman has spells for getting a husband, spells for her marriage ; spells on this side and on that ;
spells before the child is born, before the christening and after
the christening ; and all she gains with her spells is that her
child fares the worse all its life long. Ye men, it is much marvel
that ye lose not your wits for the monstrous witchcrafts that
women practise on you ! ' Priests were even known to strip
the altar of its ornaments and say a form of Mass for the death
of their enemies ; and on one occasion the monks of Winchester
Cathedral, who had a quarrel with their bishop, demonstrated
against him by going in procession the wrong way round the
church,[1] carrying their crosses upside down. The ignorant also
undoubtedly regarded images and relics of saints superstitiously.
To admire men and women who have lived good lives and given
their lives for their faith is an excellent thing ; to commemorate
them by statues is reasonable—we do the same in the streets of
our cities for the great men of the world, without even the excuse
that the results are beautiful. The Roman Church taught, and
still teaches, that prayers should be addressed to the saints, but
although it also taught that prayers made before a crucifix or
image were not made to that lifeless object but to the holy being
whom it represented, it is perfectly clear that many ignorant
persons considered the image itself holy, and worshipped it as
a heathen worships his idol. In the same way over the great
question of ' indulgences ', which led to Luther's fateful protest ;
the Pope, as successor of St. Peter, claimed the power to remit
the whole or part of the punishment due for sins, provided the
sinner was truly penitent, and the necessity for true repentance
was emphasized in many books. But in actual practice the
Pope's ' letters of indulgence ', which were hawked about the
country by ' pardoners ', men, usually of evil life, who would
sell them to any one or even stake them on a throw of the dice,
were regarded practically as licences to sin without fear of

[1] To go ' widdershins ', i.e. contrary to the course of the sun, was a
regular practice in black magic.

punishment in the next world. To put the whole matter briefly : in days before there were printed books and compulsory educa- tion, the bulk of the people necessarily depended upon their priests for religious instruction, and as the Church did not insist upon a high moral or intellectual standard for her ministers, it is not surprising that the people failed to understand these difficult spiritual matters, and interpreted them in the way that made life easiest for them.

In addition to the ordinary clergy there was a class of what we may call professional religious men and women—the monks and nuns, who withdrew themselves from the world to devote their lives to prayer and meditation. The monastic ideal of a religious community separated from the world was not peculiar to Christianity ; it was, indeed, eastern in origin, though it was introduced into Europe about the fifth century. It may be said to have had three chief aims : to save the souls of its members by avoiding the temptations of the world, to serve God by con- tinual prayer, and to serve the world by prayer and by the issue of books dealing with religion. Every monk took the three vows of poverty—none might possess property of their own ; chastity —they might not marry ; and obedience—to their superiors and to the rule of their order. The earliest and most important monastic order in western Europe was that founded by St. Benedict in 529, and introduced into England by St. Augustine in 597. The Celtic monasteries, which already existed at that date in Ireland, the Scottish Isles, and in the western, British, parts of England, were collections of religious men living, each in his own hut, near together under the control of one teacher but not under any definite rule. The Benedictines lived together, under an abbot and the officers, sharing the same buildings and observing the rules drawn up by their founder. During the early centuries, while much of Europe was still pagan, the monks were sent out as missionaries, but when once Christianity had become the established religion and the country was well sup- plied with clergy, the Benedictine order confined their members to the precincts of their monasteries.

St. Benedict

*A typical Benedictine monk : c. 1500. In the margin a beggar
with wooden leg and crutch*

Monasteries were built on a plan of which the main feature hardly ever varied. The chief building was the church, which was cruciform, the long limb of the cross being formed by the nave, the shorter upper limb by the chancel, and the side limb by the north and south transepts. At the point where the transepts met the nave and chancel was a tower. The nave separated from the rest of the church by a wooden screen, was open to the public, and often formed the church of the parish the parts east of the screen formed the monastic church, but the public were admitted to special altars and shrines within this portion. The interior of the church was planned with special reference to the processions which were a particular feature of monastic services. When the position of the church permitted the buildings of the monastery lay to the south, so as to get the sun and to have the protection of the church from the north wind; but if space was not available on that side they would be placed on the north. In any case they were grouped round an open court, the 'cloister garth', surrounded by a covered walk known as the cloisters. Most of the time of the monks that was not spent in the church was spent in the cloisters, and it was for this reason that a sunny and sheltered aspect was desirable.

One side of the cloister, as we have seen, was occupied by the church; on the opposite side lay the refectory or dining-hall. Against the wall in this cloister was the lavatory or washing trough, filled from a well in the centre of the court, or supplied by a pipe if the monastery had a system of waterworks, as the larger houses had. Inside, the refectory was much like the great hall of a private house; at one end the high table for the seniors and guests, and down the sides other tables for junior monks but instead of a musicians' gallery there was a pulpit, from which passages of the Bible or other religious works were read during meals.

The east side of the cloister contained the transept of the church, the chapter-house, in which most of the business of the monastery was transacted, and usually the parlour, a room in which the monks were allowed to meet at certain times for conversation or to receive visitors. Over the chapter-house and parlour was the dormitory or common sleeping-room ; this led at one end into the church, by a flight of steps in the transept, and at the other end into the ' rere-dorter ' or latrines. The west cloister consisted of a range of cellars on the ground-floor, with rooms above them, usually set apart for the reception of guests, as the monastery was often the hotel of the medieval traveller.

Near these main buildings was the infirmary, a large room with a chapel opening out of it. Here were the aged and infirm and sick monks, and also those who had been bled. During the Middle Ages doctors attached great importance to regular bleeding. Meals were heavy, much meat was eaten and great quantities of ale and wine drunk, and little regular exercise was taken ; men therefore became too full-blooded and liable to apoplexy and the other diseases which arise from such a condition, unless a certain amount of blood was drawn off from time to time. This was particularly necessary in the case of monks, who were tempted to eat and drink more than the average and took even less exercise, most doing no physical work beyond pottering about in the garden. Accordingly, all the monks were bled, in regular rotation, some five or six times a year, and as the process was weakening, those who had been bled were excused most of their duties for three days and allowed to retire to the infirmary, where they had light and nourishing food. The process of bleeding being simple and well known, one of the brethren could perform it, but in the case of more serious operations or illness a doctor would almost always be called in from outside, and even when a great monastery kept its own doctor, he would very rarely be a monk.

Besides the monastic buildings there would be kitchen, bakery and brewhouse, and the servants' quarters, stables, barns and wash-house. The larger houses would also have special apartments for the tailor and cobbler, and possibly a tannery, where they prepared their own leather. So that a great monastery was almost a village in itself.

The chief object of monastic life was worship. At midnigh
the monks were roused by the dormitory bell ; they at onc
rose, said their private prayers, and on the ringing of a secon
bell, descended to the church for the service of Mattins, followe
immediately by Lauds—so called because the three psalms o
praise, cxlviii–cl (each beginning with the word *Laudate*) wer
then sung. After which the brethren returned to their beds
The monastic day was reckoned from sunrise to sunset, tha
period being divided into twelve hours, which therefore varie
in length according to the season, so that the actual time of th
different services changed with the length of the day. At day
break the bell rang again ; the brethren went to the cloiste
lavatory to wash their hands and comb their hair, and the
into the church for the service of Prime, which was followed b
the morning Mass. After Mass the monks went into the chapter
house ; certain prayers and parts of the monastic rule wer
read and sometimes a sermon preached. Then the names of thos
responsible for various duties and a list of the services for the da
were read out ; after this those whose consciences accused then
of having neglected their duty confessed their faults, and thos
who had detected their brethren in wrongdoing brought thei
accusations ; those adjudged worthy of punishment were flogged
or assigned other penalties. After Chapter, the monks eithe
celebrated private Masses or sat in the cloister, reading or working
until the third hour, when the bell rang for Terce ; this servic
was followed, after a short interval, by High Mass, directly afte
which came Sext. It being now the sixth hour (i. e. midday
the brethren went into the refectory for dinner—their first mea
On ordinary days the meal would consist, in a strict house, o
bread and two courses (such as soup and meat), with fruit whe
in season. On fast days, which included every Wednesday an
Friday and all Lent, fish and eggs were eaten instead of meat
while on feasts there were additional courses and extra allow
ances of wine. Few of the wealthier houses kept strictly to fruga
fare, and in many, especially at the high table, the feeding wa
luxurious.

Cloisters : c. 1460

Apparition of the Blessed Virgin to a worshipper

After dinner the monks either went into the cloister or, in the summer, retired to the dormitory for a rest until the ninth hour, when the bell rang for None, a short service which was followed by work in the cloister or garden. About the tenth hour Evensong was sung ; then came supper, after which the brethren sat in the cloister till sunset, when they re-entered the refectory for a drink of wine, and then went into the church for Compline and thence to bed.

Such, in outline, was a typical day in a monastery, but the details would vary according to the particular Order to which the house belonged. The Benedictine Order, as we have said, was the earliest and most important, but in the course of four hundred and fifty years the strictness of the rule was a good deal relaxed. Then a wave of religious enthusiasm passing over Europe in the tenth century resulted in the establishment at Cluny in Burgundy of a reformed Order of Benedictines known as Cluniacs. In spite of the strictness of their rule the Cluniacs, who had priories in England at Lewes, Bermondsey, and else-where, soon fell away from their ideals, and became notorious for luxury. Another reformed Order, the Cistercians, was instituted by Stephen Harding at Cîteaux in 1115, and, by the influence of St. Bernard, spread rapidly over Europe, but speedily deteriorated. In their endeavour to avoid the temptations of the world, the Cistercians settled far from towns in barren moorland districts, which proved excellent for sheep, and resulted in their becoming very wealthy through their dealings in wool. Their founder had forbidden them to have stained-glass windows or any beauty of architecture in their churches, but the ruins of the magnificent Cistercian abbeys in Yorkshire—Fountains, Rievaulx, Jervais— show how completely they disobeyed his commands. Yet another reform was made by St. Bruno at the Grande Chartreuse in south-eastern France in 1086. This Carthusian rule was the strictest of all ; the monks kept practically perpetual silence, and instead of living together as a community they met only in the church and the chapter-house, each monk having his own cell to himself. The Carthusians were never numerous in

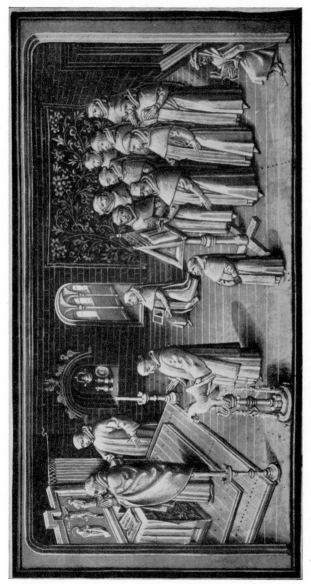

Monks in Church : c. 1460

England, but they have left their name in the London Charter-house, which after the dissolution of the monasteries became an almshouse and a great public school. They alone of the monastic Orders seem to have kept their rule unblemished.

The Benedictines and their branches were what is known as 'cloistered' Orders, their members being confined to the pre-cincts of their cloister or monastery by their rule—though in actual practice the rule was continually broken. There was, however, another Order, that of St. Augustine, in which the brethren were not so strictly confined, but were allowed to act as parish priests and in other ways to mix with the outside world. The houses of the Augustinian Order were built on the same general plan as those of the Benedictines; the religious life was practically the same, they were in the same way governed by an Abbot or Prior, but the brethren were called not monks but canons. Many of these houses of Augustinian, or Austin canons were small, and some were rather Hospitals than Priories.

Medieval hospitals were of three kinds. Some were 'lazar-houses' or leper hospitals, for persons suffering from leprosy—a name which included many skin diseases. Such diseases were common in those times, owing to the lack of personal cleanliness and the use of much salt meat and fish, with comparatively little vegetables; real leprosy was also not infrequent during the period of the Crusades, being brought back from the East. Lepers were not allowed to live in towns, and if they went through the streets to collect food and money they had to carry, and rattle, a wooden clapper to warn people of their condition, consequently leper hospitals are commonly found outside the gates of towns. Other hospitals were what we should call alms-houses, places for the aged and infirm poor, while others were nursing homes for the sick. Such was the famous hospital connected with the Austin Priory of St. Bartholomew at Smith-field, which has lasted for eight hundred years. It must not, however, be supposed that the ancient hospital of St. Bartholo-mew in any way resembled the modern 'Bart's'. The sick were

Receiving the sick and poor

Nursing the sick

Death of an inmate—his soul borne to Heaven by angels

A Hospital: c. 1250

provided with beds and food, and their spiritual wants wer
looked after by chaplains, but the attendance was kindly rathe
than skilled ; no doubt the brethren in charge obtained a certai
amount of practice in treating the simpler diseases, but n
provision was made for medical attendance, and even suc
a hospital as St. Leonard's at York, which had two hundre
beds, did not keep a resident doctor.

Another religious Order who are constantly confused with th
monks are the Friars. It is difficult to say whether the friars o
the monks would have been more annoyed by the confusion
as they were rivals who disliked and abused each other heartily
The two main Orders of Friars were the Dominicans (Friar
Preachers or Black Friars) and the Franciscans (Friars Minor
or Grey Friars), both of which were introduced into Englan
early in the reign of Henry III. Their ideals were in many way
different from those of the monks. The early monks withdrew
themselves from the world, and their houses are, therefore, ver
often in the country, away from towns : the friars went into th
world, mixing with the people and preaching to them, and there
fore their houses are always found in towns. The monks, althoug
they might not have private property, were allowed to ow
land as communities, and received so many gifts of estates tha
about a quarter of the land of England was owned by monas
teries ; the friars were not allowed to receive more land tha
was actually required for their buildings. Having no estates t
bring them in a regular income, the friars depended on the alm
of the charitable, and when the first enthusiasm for Christia
poverty had died out they neglected their religious duties fo
the pursuit of gain, and thought more of wheedling money ou
of old women for the benefit of their friary than of gaining sou
for God. There is no figure in the Middle Ages more attractiv
and lovable than St. Francis, and the first missionary friars ha
much of his spirit, but there are few figures more unpleasin
than the later medieval friars, with their greed and cunning, a
depicted in contemporary literature. Without denying that ther
were at all times good monks and friars, one cannot help seein

that both Orders had fallen a long way from their original ideals by the end of the Middle Ages, and their spiritual failure had been largely due to their worldly success. When Henry VIII turned the flame of persecution upon them, the courage with which a few monks and friars faced imprisonment and death for their faith went some way towards restoring the fallen reputation of the religious Orders.

VI

EDUCATION

HUMAN nature has changed very little since the earliest times —the nature of children as little as that of their elders—though the methods of dealing with it, encouraging good and repressing

evil tendencies, which is the purpose of education, have altered. Beginning with the first stage of life, the baby, a medieval writer's warning against married life still holds good : ' there cometh from the child thus born a wailing and a weeping that must about midnight make thee to waken ' ; and a still earlier writer is equally up-to-date in advising that a baby's eyes should be protected from the light, in insisting on the danger of impure milk, and in pointing out that a small child's limbs are liable to become bowed and bent. His method, however, of dealing with

Swaddled babies : 14th century.

this last risk, which was the method in common use for centuries, would be condemned by any modern nurse or doctor. To ensure that its limbs should grow straight the baby was swaddled, or swathed with bandages, wrapped round and round its body until it resembled a mummy or a cocoon, unable to move anything but its head ; whereas now even the restraint of long clothes is abandoned as far as possible, and the baby is encouraged to fling its arms and legs about. The same contrast is to be found between past and present methods of education. The medieval ideal of education was to bind the pupil with rules and penalties, and to push or carry him along the narrow path of learning, scarcely able to look, and quite unable to stray, to the right or left ; the modern ideal is to give the child as much freedom as possible, to encourage him to use his own brain and to love learning for its own sake. Owing to the unchanging nature of boys (and girls), neither ideal has ever had much chance of being attained very fully. It is as true now as in the twelfth century that children ' lead their lives without thought and care, and set their courages only on mirth and liking, and dread no

The Birched Schoolboy : 16th century.

perils more than beating with a rod ; and they love an apple more than gold. When they be praised, or shamed, or blamed they set little thereby. . . . They desire much meat, and so by reason of superfluity of meat and of drink they fall oft and many times into divers sicknesses and evils '. But it is no longer true that ' the more the father loveth his child, the more busily he teacheth and chastiseth him, and when the child is most loved of the father it seemeth that he loveth him not, for he beateth and grieveth him oft lest he draw to evil manners and faults '.

Severity was the key-note of medieval education ; severity in the home and severity in the school. Ill-fated Lady Jane Grey declared that her parents expected her to do everything ' even so perfitely as God made the world ' and that if she failed to reach that high standard they punished her ' with pinches, nippes and bobbes ' ; and there was nothing exceptional about Agnes Paston, who used to beat her daughter once or twice a week, and expressed the hope that if her son did not do well at school his master would ' truly be-lash him till he will amend '. It was significant that at Cambridge when a student took his degree of Master of Grammar he was given, as the symbols of his office, a birch and a palmer (a rod with a flat wooden disk at the end, used for hitting boys on the palm of the hand), and proceeded to show his fitness to act as a schoolmaster by whipping a boy provided for the purpose, who received fourpence for his pains. Occasionally a man of greater sense or humanity protested ; St. Anselm, the great Archbishop of Canterbury, pointed out that such cruelty and violence only made the boys hate their masters and everything connected with learning ; and Roger Ascham, the famous schoolmaster, when Cox of Eton was commended as the best schoolmaster and the greatest beater of his time, suggested that the success of his pupils was due rather to their ability than to his beating. In private households also the method of rewards was sometimes tried instead of punishment, as we find ' sugar plate and great comfettes (sweets) ' provided for little Francis Willoughby in 1550, ' to make hym larne his book '. But such cases were exceptional. And yet this reign of terror neither broke the spirit of medieval boys nor reduced them to angelic goodness. The poet Lydgate, writing of his boyhood in the middle of the fourteenth century, tells how he hated getting up in the morning and going to bed at night, would not wash his hands or learn his lessons, played and fought with his companions, robbed orchards, mocked at his elders and betters, played truant or came to school late and excused himself with some ingenious lie. Possibly, like the hero of an amusing fifteenth-century poem, he said his mother had sent him to milk the ducks !

My master looketh as he were mad :
' Where hast thou been, thou sorry lad ? '
' Milking ducks, as my mother bade.'
It was no marvel that I were sad ;
What availeth it me though I say nay?

〉ver the master's proceedings, against which he thus unavail-
ıg protested, it would, perhaps, be better to draw a veil. But

Boys playing at School : the ' teacher ' in the chair holds a palmer :
c. 1340.

is not surprising that the boy, sore at heart—and not only at
eart—should give vent to his feelings :

I would my master were an hare,
And all his bookës houndës were,
And I myself a jolly hunter ;
To blow my horn I would not spare !
For if he were dead I would not care.

Education is not a matter solely of book-learning. Winchester
ollege, the first of our great public schools, took as its motto,
Manners maketh man ', and a training in courtesy was recog-
ized as a necessary part of every gentleman's education. The
ɔuses of the nobles were the schools of manners, and boys were
ɛnt at an early age to the royal court or into the households
f the bishops and nobles to learn behaviour, and especially all
ıat was implied in ' table manners ', both how to behave as
guest and how to carve and serve at table. For to the medieval

mind there was nothing undignified in waiting upon a superior
indeed the right to act as butler to the king or to hold the basin
in which he washed his hands was a privilege over which nobles
would quarrel, and men of good family were proud to serve
lesser lords than the king in similar ways. Carving, in particular
was a fine art, and Chaucer names as one of the accomplishments
of his Squire that he ' carved before his father at the table '
Books of etiquette for the instruction of the young in all branches
of behaviour were common, in Latin, French, and English—one
of the best known being that called ' Stans puer ad mensam '
which Chaucer quotes in his description of the dainty way in
which his charming Prioress was wont to eat.

These books of etiquette give us a vivid picture of medieval
life, as they go carefully through all the incidents in the course
of a day in a boy's life from his getting up to his going to bed

> Ryse you early in the morning
> For it hath propertyes three,
> Holynesse, health, and happy welth,
> As my Father taught mee.

And when they say ' early ' they mean six o'clock at latest
Being up, the child is told to comb his hair, see that his shoes
and clothes are clean and properly done up, and not to forget
to wash his hands and face and say his prayers. Then come
general instructions as to behaviour ; if he is spoken to by a
superior he is to answer modestly but cheerfully, not hanging
his head ' lumpishly ' or scowling sullenly ; he is not to puff and
snort, nor to scratch himself,

> Nor imitate with Socrates
> To wipe thy snivelled nose
> Upon thy cap, as he would do,
> Nor yet upon thy clothes.

But the greater part of the work is concerned with behaviour
at table. Much of this shows that good manners have always
and in all places been the same, and may be summed up in the
idea of consideration for others : look after your neighbours, do
not grab all the best food, avoid doing anything that will offend

r disgust other people. That there was a certain lack of the
igher refinements of behaviour we may gather from its being
onsidered necessary to give such instructions as these :

> Burnish no bones with your teeth,
>   For that is unseemly ;
> Rend not thy meat asunder
>   For that swerves from curtesy.
> Dip not thy meat in the saltseller,
>   But take it with thy knyfe.
> And sup not lowde of thy Pottage,
>   No tyme in all thy lyfe.
> Defyle not thy lips with eating much,
>   As a pigge eating draffe ;
> Eate softly and drinke mannerly,
>   Take heed you do not quaffe.
> Scratche not thy head with thy fyngers
>   When thou arte at thy meate ;
> Nor spytte you over the table board ;
>   See thou doest not this forget.
> Pick not thy teeth with thy knyfe
>   Nor with thy fingers ende,
> But take a stick or some cleane thing,
>   Then doe you not offende.

Turning from the education of manners to the education of
arning, we must first notice that there were many more schools
ι medieval England than is generally realized ; in proportion
ο the population there were more schools at the beginning of
ιe fourteenth century than at the end of the eighteenth. The
omans, a very practical race, had a full appreciation of the
nportance of education ; under the later emperors schools were
umerous and schoolmasters highly paid, receiving from twelve
ο twenty times the wages of an ordinary labourer. When, in
ιe sixth century, the Church supplanted the Empire, and the
ope as head of Christendom, replaced the Emperor as head
f the civilized world, the idea of the value of education
emained, and consequently the early missionary bishops were
achers as well as preachers. A school was a necessary part
f the establishment of every ' minster ' or great church, whether
rved by monks or by ordinary clergy, in early times. We do

not know for certain that St. Augustine taught in the school
which he founded at Canterbury, but the great Theodore of
Tarsus, who became Archbishop in 669, and his companion
Abbot Hadrian, were famous as teachers. St. Aldhelm, Bishop
of Sherborne, and probable founder of Sherborne School, seems
also to have taught and was certainly a great scholar, with a knowledge of the classical authors, such as Ovid, Horace, Juvenal,
Terence, and Seneca, and of a large number of later Latin writers
whose works are no longer read. Even more famous were Bede,
master of the monastery school at Jarrow and writer of a *Church
History* which is a chief source of our knowledge of the early
history of England, and Alcuin, who was schoolmaster at York
from 776 until 782, when he became master of the Emperor
Charlemagne's Palace School.

Yet, partly owing to the disturbance of life caused by the
Danish raids, Alfred the Great in 893 had to lament the lack of
learning in England, declaring that there was hardly a man in
the South of England who could translate a letter from Latin
into English or even understand the Church service. To remedy
this, Alfred issued a number of English translations of Latin
books and did all he could to encourage schools and learning.
His example was followed by his successors, and schools grew
up all over the country. Towards the end of the tenth century
Ælfric (afterwards Abbot of Eynsham, near Oxford) wrote
several school books, of which the most interesting is a conversation in Latin, with an English translation, between a schoolmaster and his pupils. Although only written (like modern
French phrase-books) to make schoolboys familiar with common
and useful words, it is now interesting to us as showing something about an ancient school and a good deal about the life
of the time. The pupils assume the parts of a young monk,
a ploughboy, shepherd, cowherd, hunter, fisherman, merchant,
seaman, shoemaker, cook, and so forth—and each in turn gives
a description of his daily life (thus bringing in a great variety
of words and technical terms). Finally, there is an argument
as to whose work is the most valuable ; which the master decides

in favour of the ploughman, as he provides food. When the others protest against this decision, he ends by advising each to do his own work as well as he can : ' Whether you are a priest or a monk, a layman or a soldier, apply yourself to that and be what you are ; as it is a shame for a man not to be what he is and what he ought to be.'

The Norman Conquest affected education in several ways. Most important was the substitution of Norman-French for English as the language into which translation had to be done ; with the effect of this change upon the English language and literature we shall deal in another chapter, but we may note here that it was not until the middle of the fourteenth century that English (by that time very much altered) was re-introduced into schools. The Normans also favoured the monastic system, and many churches with which grammar-schools had been connected came into the hands of the monks. There were four types of schools after the Conquest : the elementary song-school, the monastic school, the grammar-school, and the university. A typical song-school is alluded to in Chaucer's delightful *Prioress's Tale*, where the ' litel clergeon, seven yeer of age ' is described as learning ' to singen and to rede, as smale childer doon in hir childhede '. At these elementary schools the boys were taught to sing Latin hymns and songs, without necessarily understanding what they meant, and learnt their ABC and reading, and possibly sometimes writing. So far as spelling was concerned, Latin was the only language that had a fixed system of spelling ; French and English were written phonetically (that is to say, the words were spelt with such groups of letters as seemed to the individual writer to represent their sound).

The monastery school was intended for boys who were going to become monks, and was therefore almost entirely concerned with religious instruction. The number of pupils, even in the large monasteries, was small and the discipline very severe ; the boys were not allowed to speak to each other or even to touch each other ; one of the older monks was assigned to each pair of boys as a teacher, and practically never let them out of

his sight, day or night. Such instruction as they received wa
mostly given in the cloister—the covered walk running round
the four sides of an open court surrounded by the monasti
buildings, which was a feature of every monastery. Occasionally
the gentry sent their sons to board in a monastery and to be
educated with the young monks, or novices, usually with the
idea that they should themselves become monks or clergy; and
some houses also kept an ' almonry ' or charity school, the boys
of which, in return for their elementary education, acted as choir
boys or servants.

The real work of education in medieval England was done by
the grammar-schools. As their name implies, their business
was to teach Latin grammar: Latin being the universal language
of learning throughout western Europe, and grammar being
defined as ' the art of speaking and writing correctly, as used
by the writers of prose and poetry '. As we have already seen,
such schools were from the earliest times a necessary part of
every cathedral and collegiate church, by which is meant a church
served by a number of canons, who were called, as were the
ordinary parish priests, ' secular ' clergy, because they mixed
with the world (Latin, *saeculum* = the world, as opposed to the
Church) in contrast to the ' regular ' clergy who lived under
a monastic rule (Latin, *regula* = a rule). In many cases during
the eleventh and twelfth centuries, as for instance at Canterbury,
Bedford, and Waltham, secular canons were replaced by regulars ;
the grammar-schools, however, continued as before, the teachers
being almost always secular clergy appointed by the monks.
In many other towns, such as St. Albans, Bury St. Edmunds,
and Lewes, there were schools taught by seculars, but under the
control of the local monastery; the monks, however, had no
more to do with the actual teaching than have the governors
of a modern public school.

A great event in the history of education was the founding
by William of Wykeham, the wealthy Bishop of Winchester,
of New College, Oxford, and, as a place in which to prepare
scholars for that college, Winchester School. The school was

ormally founded on the 20th October, 1382, though it was not ill twelve years later that the present buildings were ready for ise. There were to be seventy 'poor and needy' scholars, but rom the names of the earliest scholars, which include Wykeham's own nephew and many members of famous families, it is clear hat their poverty was only comparative, and that the founder had no idea of providing education specially for the labouring

A University Lecture : c. 1400.

classes. Winchester was not only the largest grammar-school of its time, but it was also the first school founded purely as a school and not as a branch of some ecclesiastical establishment. Sixty years later, on the 11th October, 1440, Henry VI followed Wykeham's example by founding 'the King's College of Our Lady of Eton beside Windsor', which he afterwards connected with his other foundation of King's College, Cambridge. At Eton, as at Winchester, there were 'poor and needy' scholars of good family, but Eton is the first grammar-school to be given the title of a 'public school', the meaning of which was simply that scholars might come from any part of England, and not only, as was usually the case, from the immediate neighbourhood of the school. A third foundation of the same kind was begun at the very end of our medieval period, in 1528, when Cardinal Wolsey founded a college at Oxford and a school at Ipswich ; but in 1530 Wolsey fell into disgrace, his property was seized by the king, and although Henry VIII completed the Oxford College of Christ Church, the school was suppressed.

A few years before Wolsey's educational plans were made, in 1511, Colet, Dean of St. Paul's, refounded and endowed the grammar-school which had been connected with that cathedral for probably nine hundred years. He now separated it from the control of the Dean and Chapter and put it into the hands of the Mercers' Company, so that the largest school in London was now no longer under clerical control ; moreover, the head master was a layman, and while this was not quite a new idea, seeing that as early as 1432 it was expressly ordered that the master of Sevenoaks School should not be a priest, we may see in this a kind of challenge to the monopoly of education which the Church had claimed in past times. Another mark of the growth of ' the new learning ' at this time was that Colet ordered that not only Latin but also Greek should be taught. Greek had only been introduced at Oxford in 1491, and although it had been taught at Winchester and Eton before the refounding of St. Paul's School, its inclusion by Colet among the regular subjects to be studied may be said to mark the beginning of a new period in the history of education.

Colet was also partly responsible for the issue in 1513 of Lily's *Latin Grammar*, which was made compulsory for all schools in 1528, and with very little alteration, remained without a rival for the next 350 years. Earlier medieval grammars had mostly been written in Latin verse, full of strange words, and must have been very difficult to master even when Latin was still a living language, as it was throughout the Middle Ages. Of the other books in use it is sufficient to notice that Aesop, Terence, and Virgil were used in the lower forms ; Ovid, Sallust, and Cicero

the upper. In addition to translation, essays, repetition, and
récis-writing (all, of course, in Latin) were required. The hours
ere long; at Eton, school began at 6 o'clock in the morning,
nd went on till 9, when there were prayers and quarter of an
our's interval for breakfast. Dinner was at 11; afternoon
chool from 1 to 5, except that in summer they rested until
, when they had 'bevers'—a drink of beer, which took the place

The Seven Liberal Arts : Grammar, Rhetoric, Logic, Arithmetic, Music, Geometry, and Astronomy.

f our afternoon tea. The work on Sundays was similar to that
n weekdays, but ceased at dinner-time. Only the bigger schools
ould have had more than one master, but there were assistant
ushers' for supervision duty, pupil-teachers, chosen from the
ore advanced boys, and prefects who had to report their
llows for fighting, unwashed faces, dirty clothes, failing to
lk Latin or other such breaches of discipline. Against the
ng school hours has to be set the great frequency of holy-days,
asts of the Church, on which there was either no work or only
the morning. The summer holidays at Eton, and probably
sewhere, were from Ascension Day to Corpus Christi (the

Thursday after Trinity Sunday); there were also holidays a
Christmas and sometimes at Easter, and during the harves
season.

Though there were no organized games as in modern school
there were plenty of games of one kind and another. Ball game
resembling (more or less) hockey, fives, tennis, and rounder
were played, the walls of churches being often chosen as fives
courts, to the considerable injury of the windows. Football wa
also a favourite game, and the three schools of London—thos
of St. Paul's, St. Mary-le-Bow, and St. Martin-le-Grand—use
to assemble on the open ground of Smithfield to play footba
in the afternoon on Shrove Tuesday. The morning of Shrov
Tuesday was given up to cock-fighting, the boys bringing the
game-cocks to school and matching them against one another
this amusement, sufficiently barbarous in itself, degenerated i
later times into the practice of tying a cock to a post and throw
ing sticks at it until the unfortunate bird was killed, and suc
Shrove Tuesday cock-throwing was practised, with the encourage
ment of the masters, down to Puritan days. But if mediev
boys indulged in brutality for which a modern boy would l
deservedly kicked by his companions, they also indulged in a
intellectual form of amusement, for which, one cannot hel
thinking, a modern boy would run some risk of being undeserved
kicked ; this was the practice of assembling in some public plac
in the streets, on a holiday, to dispute in Latin with rival schola
on points of grammar or of logic.

This intellectual keenness was due to the fact that the schoo
taught not only grammar but also logic (the art of arguing) an
rhetoric (the art of public speaking). These three subjec
formed the *Trivium*, or threefold path of learning, with whic
most educated people were content ; but scholars, who despis
such ' trivial ' learning, would go on to the fourfold *Quadriviu*
of arithmetic, geometry, music, and astronomy. It may see
strange that arithmetic should be regarded as one of the mo
advanced and less necessary subjects of education, but it mu
be remembered that it was not until the fourteenth centu

COLLEGIUM MERTONENSE

Merton College, Oxford

that Arabic numerals began to come into use, and the processe
of arithmetic with Roman numerals were far from simple. The
learned Bishop Aldhelm, when he took up mathematics, wrote
' The despair of doing sums oppressed my mind so that all the
previous labour spent on learning seemed nothing. At last, by
the help of God's grace, I grasped, after incessant study, tha
which lies at the base of reckoning :—what they call fractions.

During the twelfth century groups of advanced schools, wher
lectures on the more difficult branches of learning were given
began to grow up in many places, as for instance at Paris and
at Bologna in Italy. These communities of scholars and teacher
came to be known as ' universities '. For some unknown reason
such a university grew up at Oxford, and by the end of th
reign of Henry I it had become sufficiently important to attrac
lecturers from Paris and Bologna, while by the end of the twelft
century Oxford had become the recognized centre of learning i
England. Cambridge followed a little later, and by the middl
of the thirteenth century both universities were firmly estab
lished, with a system of laws and officials, of whom the hea
was the Chancellor. The students at first lived in such room
as they could get in the town. Gradually the custom grew u
of a number of students living together in one house, or ' hall '
under the control of a master or principal. The next step wa
for some of these halls to be endowed ; that is to say for som
wealthy person to grant lands, of which the rents were used fo
the support of the hall and the students living in it, the grantc
at the same time laying down certain rules for the governanc
of the hall. Such an endowed and regulated hall was known a
a ' college ', the first college being that founded at Oxford b
Walter de Merton in 1263.

There was no very distinct line between the grammar-schoo
and the university. Boys might come up to the university a
the age of thirteen or fourteen, though seventeen was a mor
usual age, and the less advanced pupils could continue to stud
grammar there. The teaching of the more advanced subject
of which theology and law were the most important, was b

means of lectures given by Masters of Arts, and the candidate for the degree of Bachelor of Arts did not, as he does now, have to pass an examination, but only to produce certificates that he had attended a certain number of courses of lectures and that his teachers considered him worthy of a degree. If he wished to go on to the degree of Master of Arts he must study for another three years ; at the end of which time he displayed his learning by carrying on a disputation with other Masters, gave a banquet to the other Masters, and was duly invested with the degree. Every Master of Arts was definitely a teacher, and as such was bound to give courses of lectures ; and this, it may be remarked, was not always a pleasant task, as the medieval student was lively and ill-mannered and had no scruples about ragging and howling down an unpopular lecturer. Lecturers were not the only sufferers from the high spirits of the students ; the unfortunate freshman, known as a ' bajan ' (French, *bec jaune* = yellow-beak, i.e. callow bird), had to submit to all kinds of indignities and horseplay at the hands of his elders, who pretended to regard him as a horrible wild beast with horns and long beard, which had to be cut off. Nor were they content with such comparatively harmless displays of unruliness ; in spite of frequent prohibitions, the students often wore swords and daggers, and had no hesitation in using them in quarrels between rival factions (the students from the north and south of England were constantly fighting each other) or against the townsmen in ' town and gown ' riots, in which the casualties on both sides were very heavy. Altogether, it is clear that in the Middle Ages a university education may have led to an increase of learning, but did not tend to mildness of manners.

VII

LITERATURE

THE language of the Anglo-Saxons was what is called an ' inflected ' language, that is to say a language, like Latin or German, in which the case of a noun or adjective is shown by the form of its case-ending ; whereas in modern English the only case-ending is the 's of the genitive—we can say either ' the king's land ' or ' the land of-the-king ', but for the dative we must say ' to-the-king ' and we cannot tell whether ' the king ' is nominative or accusative without looking at the rest of the sentence. Anglo-Saxon nouns also had genders with which the adjectives had to agree, and altogether it was much like German ; the two languages were, in fact, closely related, the Angles and Saxons being branches of the great ' Teutonic ' race, of which the ancestors of the Germans were also branches. Yet another branch were the Scandinavians of Denmark, Norway, and Iceland. Nor was it only in the form of their languages that these peoples resembled each other : their ideas and traditions as shown in their poetry, were very similar. The one subject which they thought worthy of the poet's attention was war their heroes were fierce warriors, who fought and plundered and feasted ; their speeches are usually an exchange of insults and the scenery in which they are set is pictured as barren desolate, and grim. The earliest and most famous Anglo-Saxon

---

[1] As an illustration of Anglo-Saxon we may take a sentence from the will of Alfred the Great : ' minum twam sunum an thusend punda aegthrum fif hund punda ; and minre yldstan dehter, and thaere mede mestan, and thaere gingstran and Ealhswithe, him feowrum feower hund punda, aelcum an hund punda ' [' to my two sons a thousand pounds to either five hundred pounds ; and to my eldest daughter and to the midmost and to the youngest and to Ealhswith, to the four of them four hundred pounds, to each a hundred pounds ']. If this sentence is read out omitting the case-inflections at the ends of most of the words, it will be found to resemble the modern English of the translation pretty closely.

poem, 'Beowulf', is a story concerned not with England but with Denmark, and its hero's combats with half-human monsters are very like the struggle of Grettir and Glam (one of the finest of all ' ghost stories ') in the Scandinavian saga of Grettir. Even when later Anglo-Saxon poets wrote on Christian religious subjects they kept much of their old gloom and ferocity ; their saints are God's warriors, bent on punishing sin, and storms, war, and the terrors of hell are the incidents most vividly described. As their language was unaffected by that of the conquered Britons, so their literature was untouched by the Celtic love of beauty and romance.

Anglo-Saxon prose is closely associated with the name of Alfred the Great. In the last chapter we have seen that he lamented the decay of learning in England. He was only a moderately good Latin scholar himself ; this was fortunate, as instead of writing books in Latin and helping to make that the only literary language (as it was in France), he encouraged the use of English, and himself issued several translations into that language. His translations, as a rule, were very free ; with the aid of Archbishop Plegmund, Bishop Asser, and other learned men, he got the general sense of his Latin author and then put it into his own words, omitting what he considered unnecessary, and occasionally adding matter of his own. Most of these additions are moral reflections, but into the history text-book of Orosius he introduces the earliest account of an Arctic expedition, as he received it himself from Ohthere, a Norwegian explorer who had sailed as far as the White Sea. To Alfred also we owe the great Anglo-Saxon Chronicle ; in this were collected the traditions of the Anglo-Saxons from the time of their landing in Britain down to his own time ; copies of the Chronicle were apparently given to the more important monasteries and were kept up to date, the Peterborough copy being continued right down to the accession of Henry II in 1154. Such a Chronicle, written in the language of the country, is unique—no other nation can show anything similar : for the most part it consists solely of entries of events—the death of such a king, the ravages of the

Danish pirates, records of exceptional frosts and tempests, an
so on—without comment, and is history rather than literatur
but occasionally the chronicler is moved to greater efforts
Athelstan's great victory of ' Brunanburh ' in 938 is recorded i
a long and spirited battle-chant, not unlike the Song of Debora
and Barak in the Old Testament, and the deaths of Edgar an
Edward the Confessor are both treated poetically. There

The Anglo-Saxon Chronicle.

also a fine word-picture of William the Conqueror, containi
the oft-quoted phrase, ' he loved the tall deer as if he were the
father ', and a famous dramatic description of the terrible da
of King Stephen, when ' men said openly that Christ and h
saints were asleep '.

The Norman Conquest had a very great influence upon Englis
literature. It affected language, ideas, and methods of expre
sion. The Normans were by descent, as their name show
Northmen—Scandinavians, from the same Teutonic stock as th
Saxons ; they had been established in France barely two hundre
years at the time of the Conquest, but their language ha

Chaucer

Reading his poems to a fashionable audience : c. 1390

practically disappeared, and they now spoke the language of the conquered French, while the Anglo-Saxons still spoke the language of their ancestors, very little changed during the five centuries that had passed since their arrival in England. Under the Norman kings French became the polite language of England ; Latin was, as it had been and as it continued to be till the end of the Middle Ages, the language of the Church and of the learned throughout Europe, but English was spoken only by the poorer and uneducated people. One trace of this fact can be seen in our own speech ; the live animals of the farmyard are called by the Saxon names given them by the peasants who had to look after them—oxen, sheep, swine; but when cooked for the master's table they take on French names—beef, mutton, pork. And the fact that modern English is a blend of words derived mainly from Saxon and French sources is chiefly due to the Conquest ; so also is the disappearance of inflections and genders. Conversation between the Normans and their Saxon subjects was presumably carried on in a blend of broken English and French, in which the inflections of both languages would be maltreated or ignored ; and as, even among the natives the inflections (case-endings, &c.) varied in the different dialects, the tendency would be to drop them. So, too, in this confusion of tongues, it was not easy to be sure of the gender of a noun when the gender had nothing to do with the nature of the thing ; consequently modern English is the only language which has a reasonable system of genders : in Anglo-Saxon ' a wife ' was neuter, in German it still is, but in English she is feminine, and while a Frenchman has to say *son chapeau* whether he is talking of a man's top-hat or of his wife's latest creation, the Englishman does not worry about the gender of ' hat ', but thinks of the much more important question of its owner, and says ' his ' or ' her hat '.

This blending of English and French into a single simplified language was not a rapid process. For some three centuries after the Conquest the two languages continued in use side by side, each absorbing more and more words from the other, until about 1350, when, partly owing to the growth of a national feeling of patriotism at the beginning of the great struggle with France ('The Hundred Years' War'), English began to gain the upper hand and re-appeared in the schools, the law-courts, and the houses of the gentry. Trevisa, writing at the end of the fourteenth century, says :

' John Cornwaile, a maister of grammer, chaunged the lore in gramer scole and construccioun of Frensche in to Englische ; and Richard Pencriche lerned that manere of techynge of hym, and other men of Pencrich ; so that now, the yere of our Lorde a thowsande thre hundred and foure score and fyve, in alle the gramere scoles of Englond children leveth Frensche and construeth and lerneth in Englische, and haveth thereby avauntage in oon side and disavauntage in another side ; here avauntage is that they lerneth the gramer in lesse tyme than children were i-woned to doo; disavauntage in that now children of gramer scole conneth no more Frensche than can their left heele, and that is harme for hem and (=if) they schulde passe the see and travaille in straunge lands and in many other places. Also gentil men haveth now moche i-left for to teche their children Frensche.'

Three great figures stand out in the literature of this period— the author of *Piers Plowman*, Chaucer, and Wycliffe.

The author of *The Vision concerning Piers Plowman* is usually said to have been Will Langland, born in the neighbourhood of Malvern about the beginning of the reign of Edward III, but nothing is really known about him. The poem, however, is extremely interesting in many ways : it is a long, and rather confused, allegory of man's search for Truth, not unlike Bunyan's *Pilgrim's Progress*, told in a series of dreams, which begin ' on a May morning on Malvern hills '. In his visions the dreamer passes continually through crowds—such crowds as might be seen at a fair or in a market-town—and his pictures of the different scenes are wonderfully vivid ; his description of the company in a tavern we have already quoted, and the whole book is full of such pictures. The whole is a satire or a sermon against the corruption of the court, the government, and the Church, and social conditions generally, as they were at the end of the reign of the

old King Edward III and at the beginning of the reign of the boy
King Richard II. He denounces the prevalence of bribery and
greed of money, the lawyers who will defend the wealthy evil
doer and oppress the poor, good man, the clergy and friar
who are more anxious to extort money from their flock than to
save their souls, and above all he denounces idleness, whether
in the rich or the poor ; his hero is Piers the Plowman, who
works honestly to cultivate the land and grow crops, not for
his own enrichment but to feed the people, and it is in the guise
of the Plowman that he portrays Christ. Although he was
severe towards the idle poor, who sit about and sing vulgar
songs instead of working, his denunciations of their oppressors
caused him to be hailed as the champion of the labouring classes,
and during the Peasants' Rising of 1381 quotations from the
poem are found in the mouths of the leaders of that revolt
though it is clear that he would not have approved of that
rising or of the socialist and heretical ideas of the Lollards.

Apart from its subject-matter, *Piers Plowman* is interesting
for the manner in which it is written. The poetry is of the Old
English style—the style that was used in *Beowulf*. The early
Anglo-Saxons rarely made use of rhyme (which is the repetition
of similar sounds at the end of each of two or more lines), but
used ' alliteration ' (which is the repetition of the same letter at
the beginning of a number of words which come near together).
In their poems each line was divided into two halves ; each half
contained two accented syllables—two syllables on which, when
they were recited, more emphasis was laid than on the others—
and of these, two in the first half and one in the second half of
the line had to begin with the same letter. As illustrations we
may take one or two lines from *Piers Plowman* : at the beginning
of his vision the dreamer looks out over a landscape in which is

> A *d*epe *d*ale benethe, | a *d*ongeon there-inne,
> With depe *d*yches and *d*arke | and *d*redful of sight.

Beyond this is a great plain, ' a field full of folk ', where he sees
crowds

> Of alle *m*aner of *m*en, | the *m*ean and the riche.

Of this purely English form of poetry, *Piers Plowman* is one of the most interesting pieces. To about the same period belongs a poem called *Sir Gawayne and the Green Knight*, in

King Arthur and his Round Table.
The Vision of the Holy Grail.

which a romantic story of King Arthur's court is told, with much grace and vigour, in this same alliterative verse ; and yet it can hardly be considered so purely English, for the subject is foreign, the Arthurian legend had returned into England from France. The very word ' romance ' with its double meaning of, first, ' one of the languages (such as French,

Spanish, or Italian) derived from the Romans ', and then ' a picturesque story of the kind popular in romance-speaking countries ', marks such a story as different from those of the Anglo-Saxons. Moreover, *Sir Gawayne* makes a further break away from the English tradition, as at the end of each stanza of about twenty lines of alliterative verse there are four short lines of rhymed verse. Another poem, probably by the author of *Sir Gawayne*, is *The Pearl*, a beautiful and touching lament of a father for his dead daughter, which is not only French in its loving description of the beauties of Nature, but is entirely in rhymed verse, though it contains much alliteration.

The Battle of Hastings is said to have begun with the Norman knight Taillefer riding forward alone, singing the song of the Death of Roland at Roncesvaux. The incident was significant for the history of English poetry. The *Chanson de Roland* was the greatest of the French romantic poems ; and as the English went down before the Normans on the field of Hastings, so English alliterative verse was destined to give way to the romance and rhymed verse of France ; but in neither case was the victory lightly won. Rhyme had originated in Latin songs at an early date and had soon spread to the French language ; it is even found to a small extent in the later poetry of the Anglo-Saxons. The latter also upon occasion used ' assonance ', an incomplete form of rhyme in which only the *vowel* sounds of the words that end the lines are similar. ' Assonance ' has continued in use in the popular poetry of folk-songs and nursery rhymes, and may be illustrated by one of the latter :

> Little Tommy Tucker
> Sang for his supper.
> What shall we give him ?
> Brown bread and butter.

It was, however, a result of the Norman Conquest that rhyme became the recognized method of writing English poetry, and it was in Chaucer's hands that medieval English rhymed verse reached its highest point.

Geoffrey Chaucer, born about 1340, was the son of a London

vine merchant, and was in the medieval equivalent of the Civil
Service ; he was at various times controller of the customs,
clerk of the works, commissioner of
roads, a member of Parliament, and
several times employed on diplomatic
missions to Flanders, France, and
Italy; in addition to which he served
in the army in France, being on one
occasion taken prisoner. He was,
therefore, evidently a capable man of
business, who had mixed with all classes
of society and seen something of the
two romance lands of Italy and France,
both of which were admittedly superior
to England in literature. Moreover,
he was born just at the time when, as
we have said, English was making good
its position as the spoken and written
language of all classes. The circumstances of his life and of his times
combined to assist the poetic genius of
his nature, and he became the greatest
literary figure of medieval England
and second only to Shakespeare in the
roll of English poets. His early work
was very much under French influence,
some of the pieces, such as the *Romance
of the Rose*, being actual translations
from the French and others being
adaptations. He next fell under the
spell of Italy, especially of Boccaccio,
the brilliant writer of tales and poems
of love and romance. The chief poem

Chaucer.

of this second period is *Troilus and Criseyde*—based on a poem of
Boccaccio's which tells the love-story of the Trojan prince Troilus
and the fickle Criseyde, a story which had been used before by

several writers, and was used again by Shakespeare for his play, *Troilus and Cressida*. The way in which both English poets introduced fresh beauties and particularly the charm of humour is a good proof that what is essential in a poem is not the story but the telling of it. Apart from its being delightful to read (with judicious skipping, for it suffers from the medieval failing of long-windedness), *Troilus and Criseyde* is important as being written in ' rhyme royal '—possibly so called from its afterwards being used by the royal poet, James I of Scotland : in this the poem is built up of stanzas or sections, each consisting of seven lines, each containing ten syllables, the first line rhyming with the third, the second with the fourth and fifth, and the sixth with the seventh (the rhymes may be represented graphically by *a b a b b c c*). To take an instance from the beginning of the *Troilus* :

> And so bifel, when comen was the tyme
> Of Aperil, when clothéd is the mede
> With newé grene, of lusty Ver the pryme,
> And sweté smellen flourés whyte and rede,
> In sondry wyses shewéd, as I rede,
> The folk of Troye hir (= their) observaunces olde,
> Palladiones festé for to holde.

Chaucer had experimented with ' rhyme royal ' before, but we may say that it was from the time of *Troilus* that it took its place—a place which it held for the next two hundred years—as a favourite metre of English poetry.

Chaucer's final, purely English, period is that of *The Canterbury Tales*. In this work he brings together, from many different sources, a number of stories of widely varying kinds. As a framework to hold these stories together he brings to the Tabard Inn at Southwark nine-and-twenty persons who are preparing to ride on pilgrimage to the shrine of St. Thomas Becket at Canterbury, and makes them agree to tell stories as they ride, to pass the time. The Prologue, in which he describes all the members of the party, is a series of character sketches that for vividness and humour have never been surpassed in English literature.

he company are of all ranks of society—a Knight, the very
ype of all that was best in chivalry, his gay and gallant son,
 delightful Prioress, dainty and charming, with three priests
ttending her, a fat Monk, more fond of sport than of psalm-
inging, a wily Friar, a Merchant, a learned Clerk of Oxford,
 drunken Cook, a Shipman with a taste for piracy, a poor
'arson, who both taught Christ's law and followed it himself,
 sturdy, red-bearded Miller, a Reeve, and others, including the
Iost of the Tabard Inn, Chaucer himself, and that wonderful
voman the Wife of Bath. Not only does Chaucer draw every
ne of these with unfailing skill, but he makes them act con-
istently throughout; the tales they tell and their comments
n those told by others are absolutely in keeping with their
haracters. The Knight begins with one of the romances so
opular in courtly circles in the Middle Ages; the next should
e the Monk, but the Miller, being drunk, insists on telling
 coarse and vulgar story, of which the butt is a carpenter;
his angers the Reeve, who was a carpenter by trade, and he
etorts with an equally vulgar tale about a miller. Chaucer
pologizes for the coarseness of these stories and of some of the
thers, laying the blame on the coarse nature of the tellers, and
nakes amends with such delightful stories as that which he puts
nto the mouth of the Prioress. Chaucer's own contribution is
wofold; when called upon for a tale he begins with ' Sir
Thopas ', which is a neat parody of popular romances, dragging
n interminably and full of wordy nothingness: at last the Host
an stand it no longer, and bids him stop his silly rhymes and
alk sense: he complies by telling the ' Tale of Melibeus ' in
rose; apparently it was appreciated by his hearers, but most
nodern readers find it very boring. The Monk follows with
 whole series of historic instances of the way in which the
nighty have fallen into misfortune, from Lucifer down to King
Croesus—very edifying but depressing, so that most of the
ompany are reduced almost to sleep, and the Knight politely
ut firmly insists upon his stopping. The Host calls upon one
f the Prioress's priests, and he responds with the gayest of all

the tales—that of Chaunteclere, the cock, Dame Pertilote, hi
wife, and the fox, which is a perfectly delightful version o
a very old story.

Of Chaucer's contemporaries, John Gower was the mos
notable ; he wrote, with ability, three long poems, one in Latin
one in French, and one in English, a fact which helps us to
remember that literature in England was still tri-lingual—every
one with any pretence at education spoke the three languages
John Lydgate and Thomas Occleve were industrious poets who
wrote a little after Chaucer in point of time, but a long way
after him in point of merit, and the Chaucerian tradition wa
best kept up by the Scottish poets of the fifteenth century—
King James I, Robert Henryson, William Dunbar, and Gavin
Douglas—all of whom exhibit a vigour and originality which is
lacking in the contemporary English poets.

As *Piers Plowman* represents the old English alliterative
poetry and Chaucer the new English rhymed verse, so Wycliffe
may stand for English prose. John Wycliffe, born in Yorkshire
about 1320, went up to Oxford, where he soon became prominent
as a lecturer on theology. Like Langland and Chaucer he saw
and deplored the greed and corruption of the Church, but he
was not content to meet it with satire or ridicule ; he aimed at
its reformation by placing the Church more under the control of
the State, lessening the power of the Pope, removing the tempta-
tion of wealth from the clergy, and above all, basing religion upon
the Bible. For this purpose he undertook the translation of the
Bible into English. Up to this time no complete version had
been issued, and even such parts as had been translated were
only grudgingly allowed in the hands of the laity—nor did the
Church support his scheme for making the Scriptures widely
known ; on the contrary, such knowledge in a layman was
considered almost a proof of heresy. From a literary point of
view the importance of Wycliffe's work lies in its being the first
complete version of the book which, more than any other book,
has influenced English literature, and in its containing the germ
of that Authorized Version (of 1611) in which English prose

Occleve

presenting his works to Prince Hal : c. 1410

reached the very highest point which it ever attained. To show how far the Wycliffite and Authorized versions resemble one another, and in what ways the language of 1380 differed from that of 1611, we may take the well-known passage at the beginning of the Gospel of St. Mark :

'The bigynnynge of the gospel of Jhesu Crist, the sone of God. As it is writun in Ysaie, the prophete, Lo ! I sende myn angel bifore thi face, that schal make thi weye redy bifore thee. The voyce of oon cryinge in desert, Make ye redy the weye of the Lord, make ye his pathis rightful. Jhon was in desert baptisynge, and prechinge the baptym of penaunce, in to remiscioun of synnes. And alle men of Jerusalem wenten out to him, and al the cuntre of Judee ; and weren baptisid of him in the flood of Jordan, knowlechinge her synnes. And John was clothid with heeris of camelis, and a girdil of skyn abowte his leendis ; and he eet locustus, and hony of the wode, and prechide, seyinge : A strengere than I schal come aftir me, of whom I knelinge am not worthi for to undo the thwong of his schoon.'

The period at which Wycliffe and his assistants (for his translation of the Bible was not undertaken single-handed) were working was one in which other translators flourished—notably John Trevisa, a Cornish priest, chaplain to Lord Berkeley, by whose encouragement he was persuaded to translate Higden's *Polychronicon*, a popular history of the world. When Trevisa suggested putting it into verse, the favourite medium for such works, Lord Berkeley very sensibly insisted that it should be 'In prose, for comynlich prose is more clere than ryme, more esy and more pleyn to knowe and understonde '. The result justified Lord Berkeley, as it is a lively rendering in vigorous, colloquial English. Trevisa also translated Bartholomew's book *Of the Nature of Things*, a famous medieval encyclopaedia of natural history. As an example of his prose we may take his description of the Cat :

'The catte is a beaste of uncerten heare (=hair) and colour ; for some catte is white, some rede, some blacke, some skewed (=piebald) and speckled in the fete and in the face and in the eares. And he is . . . in youth swyfte, plyaunte, and mery, and lepeth and reseth (=rusheth) on all thynge that is to-fore him ;

and is led by a strawe and playeth therwith. And is a right hevy beast in age, and ful slepy, and lieth slily in wait for myce . . . and when he taketh a mous he playeth therwith, and eateth him after the play. . . . And he maketh a rutheful noyse and gastfull when one proffereth to fyghte with another.'

From which we may see that cats have changed not at all, and English prose (apart from spelling) not greatly since 1396.

The development of English prose was carried on during the fifteenth century by such writers as Reynold Pecock, Bishop of Chichester, whose logical defence of the Church against the Lollards led to his own condemnation as a heretic ; Sir John Fortescue, Chief Justice under Henry VI, whose *Monarchy*, a book in praise of constitutional monarchy, was the first work of the kind ; and Sir Thomas Malory. The last named wrote in 1469 the *Morte d'Arthur*, an English version of the French legends of King Arthur ; his style is extraordinarily simple and straightforward, probably no writer ever used fewer adjectives, and yet he is wonderfully successful in telling his story and holding his readers' attention. As an example we may take an adventure of Sir Lancelot, when he rode disguised in the armour of Sir Kay the Seneschal :

'Sir Launcelot rode into a deepe forrest, and there by a glade he saw foure knights hoving (=loitering) under an oke, and they were of king Arthurs court ; that one was Sagramour le Desirous, sir Ector de Maris, sir Gawaine and sir Ewaine. Anon as these foure knights had spied sir Launcelot, they wend by his arms it had been sir Kay. "Now, by my faith," said sir Sagramour, "I will prove sir Kayes might"; and gat his speare in his hand and came toward sir Launcelot. Thereof was sir Launcelot ware, and knew him well, and fewtred his speare against him and smote sir Sagramour so sore that horse and man fel to the earth. . . .

'*Led by a strawe.*'

" Now I well see ", said sir Gawaine, " I must encounter with that knight." And so he dressed his shield and got a good speare in his hand, and sir Launcelot knew him well ; and then they let their horses run as fast as they might, and either smote other on the middest of their shields ; but sir Gawaines speare brake, and sir Launcelot charged so sore upon him that his horse reversed up-so-doune ; and much sorrow had sir Gawaine to avoide his horse ; and so sir Launcelot passed on a pace and smiled, and said : " God give him joy that this speare made, for there came never a better in my hand." '

A contrast to Malory may be found in Sir John Bourchier, Lord Berners, who translated the picturesque *Chronicles* of Froissart into a florid English which suits these romantic tales of chivalry. Take as an instance the opening of the battle of Crecy by the Genoese crossbowmen :

' When the French kyng sawe the Englysshmen, his blode chaunged and he sayde to his mershals : " Make the Genowayes go on before, and begynne the batyl in the name of God and saynt Denyse." Ther were of the Genowayes crosbowes about a fiftene thowsand, but they were so wery of goyng a fote that day a six leages armed with their crosbowes, that they sayd to the constables : " We be not wel ordred to fyght this day, for we be not in the case to do any great dede of armes, we have more nede of rest." These wordes came to the erle of Alanson, who sayd, " A man is well at ease to be charged with suche a sorte of rascalles, to be faynt and fayle now at moost nede." Also the same season there fell a great rayne and a clyps with a terryble thonder and before the rayne there came fleyng over bothe batayls a great nombre of crowes, for feare of the tempest commynge. Then anone the eyre beganne to waxe clere, and the sonne to shyne fayre and bright, the which was right in the Frenchmens eyen and on the Englysshmens backes. When the Genowayes were assembled toguyder, and beganne to aproche, they made a great leape and crye to abasshe thenglysshemen, but they stode styll and styredden not for all that. Then the Genowayes agayne the seconde tyme made another leape and a fell crye, and stepped forwarde a lytell, and thenglysshmen removed not one fote. Thirdly agayne they leapt and cryed, and went forth tyll they came within shotte ; then they shotte feersly with their crosbowes. Then thenglysshe archers stept forthe one pase, and lette flye their arrowes so holly and so thycke that it eemed snowe.   When the Genowayes felte the arowes persynge hrough heads, armes and brestes, many of them cast downe their rosbowes and dyd cutte their strynges and retourned dysconfited.'

Our sketch of English prose may end with William Caxton, who stablished the first printing-press in England in 1476, and not only printed several of the books we have mentioned but was also an author and translator himself, and in one of his works—

his translation of the Aeneid —alludes to the way in which English had altered even in his own time :
 'Certaynly our langage now used varyeth farre from that whiche was used and spoken when I was borne.' But, thanks largely to the invention of printing, by which identical copies of books were spread all over the country, so lessening local eccentricities of dialect and producing uniformity of language, the changes since Caxton's days have been comparatively slight ;

Printer's mark of Caxton.

four hundred years before Caxton the natives of England were speaking pure Anglo-Saxon, four hundred years after his time they were using a language which differed little from his own, except in pronunciation.

In this sketch of the development of English literature we have only been able to touch on works of outstanding importance.   Behind this there is a great mass of popular literature—stories, ballads, love-songs, carols, hymns, comic songs, political skits, sermons—much of it interesting, beautiful or amusing, with which it is impossible to deal here.   But a few words must be given to the history of the drama.   The dramatic

art, which had risen to its height in ancient Greece, and ha
continued to exist under the Romans, was swept away by th
barbarians at the break-up of the Roman Empire. When i
rose again it was, as it had been in Greece, in connexion wit
religion. The representation in the churches at Christmas o
Easter of the Nativity or Resurrection, at first in dumb show
but soon with a certain amount of dialogue, developed int
regular plays, and other scenes of biblical history or from th
legends of the saints were acted. So popular were the play
that more room was required for the audience, so they wer
acted on platforms in the churchyard. From pious representa
tions of sacred history they developed into crudely realisti
dramas, enlivened with comic relief, often vulgar and eve
indecent ; the dignitaries of the Church denounced them i
vain. The next step was that in the towns the plays were take
over by the gilds and were acted in the streets and open space
on the feast of Corpus Christi. For this purpose ' pageants '—
movable platforms on wheels—were employed ; these wer
often of two stories, the lower hung round with curtains, formin
a dressing-room for the actors, the upper being the stage. Scener
there was practically none, except occasionally a painted back
cloth, but there were various ' properties ', the most importan
being ' Hell mouth ', a huge painted canvas dragon's head, fron
which issued smoke and flames and comic devils, and into whic
the wicked were thrust. The plays, which ranged throug
sacred history from the Creation of the World to the Day o
Judgement, were assigned to definite gilds, often with som
appropriateness : the shipbuilders would play Noah's Ark, th
goldsmiths the Adoration of the Magi, the wine-merchants th
Marriage at Cana, and so on. A good many of the plays hav
survived, and some of them show considerable dramatic power
especially where the characters are peasants—such as the shep
herds in the Nativity or St. Joseph. Joseph, it may be observed
was usually treated with scant respect ; in fact the freedom
with which the composers of these plays treated their subject
and their characters is astonishing to the modern mind. On

Staging of a Miracle Play: 16th century

Showing on the right the mouth of Hell

Nativity play opens with a scene of real comedy in which one character steals a sheep, and when the shepherds come to search his house, hides it in a cradle and pretends it is his new-born son ; in another, when the angels have sung *Gloria in Excelsis*, the shepherds burlesque their singing ; Herod and Pilate were stock comic characters—blustering, ranting, swaggering bullies, and Noah's wife caused roars of laughter by her continual refusal to come into the Ark, and her boxing Noah's ears when he drags her aboard. Yet mixed with all this low comedy were passages of real pathos and simple beauty, and behind it lay a national feeling for the dramatic which was to find its expression in the Elizabethan dramatists, culminating in the genius of Shakespeare.

VIII

ART AND SCIENCE

ARCHITECTURE may claim to be the first of the arts, as some
nd of a house is the first requirement of civilized man, at least
 such a climate as ours. And the first problem of architecture
 the covering of open spaces. It is a simple matter to build
ur walls with mud or wood or stones, but not quite so simple
 roof in the space so enclosed; it is easy enough to leave
aces in your walls for doors and windows, but not quite so
sy to carry up the walls above those spaces. If the space to
: bridged is small and there are long pieces of stone or wood
ailable, one of these long pieces can be put across the top of
e window, or in the case of a roof a number of them can be
it across the narrower way of the room at intervals with
orter pieces laid across them. The disadvantages of this style
 building are, first, that long pieces of stone or wood are hard
 get and heavy to handle, and secondly, that if they have
uch weight to carry—a high wall above the window or a heavy
ll of snow on the roof—the long pieces are liable to break in
e middle, where they have no support. It was soon found
iat by cutting blocks of stone slightly wedge-shaped they
uld be fitted together to form a semi-circular arch; if such
i arch were placed over a door or window the weight of the
all above it would press upon the centre stone of the arch,
hich would pass on the pressure to those on either side of it,
id they in turn to their neighbours, until the whole weight
ime eventually to rest at the ends of the semicircle, which
ere supported by the solid wall on either side of the window.
 By constructing a continuous series of such round arches it is
issible to roof in a narrow building, and such 'barrel vaults'
o called from their resembling a barrel cut down the middle)
e found in some early Norman churches and castles. But if
 broad space has to be bridged the weight of the barrel vault

is so great that the walls have to be of enormous thickn
to support it. Roofs were, therefore, usually made of wo
The principles of constructing a wooden roof are as follo
at each end of the building and at regular intervals betwe
the ends are set pairs of beams, one end of each beam rest
on the side wall and the other ends meeting at an angle abo
the space to be roofed in ; these beams at their angle of meet
carry, and are connected together by, ' a ridge-beam ', runn
parallel to the length of the building ; across the beams
nailed planks or laths (strips of wood), and the whole is th
covered with some wet-resisting substance, such as lead, til
or thatch. The weight of the roof is thus carried by these pa
of beams and tends to thrust the ends that rest on the wa
outwards ; there were two ways to prevent this ; in sm
houses the beams, instead of resting on the walls, were ma
out of huge pieces of curved timber, of which the lower er
rested on the ground and were quite independent of the walls
in large buildings the ends of the beams were held together
a massive ' tie-beam ' running across from one wall to the oth
Further solidity was given to the construction (as can be se
by a glance at the roof of almost any church) by an uprig
' king-post ' set in the middle of the tie-beam and giving
' braces ' to the beams ; sometimes instead of a central kir
post the tie-beam carries a pair of ' queen-posts ', equidista
from the centre. Many additions, structural and ornament
were made to this design, so that a medieval wooden roof v
often a very elaborate and beautiful structure, but under
the carving and decoration the essential principles remain
the same.

The whole development of architecture may be said to ha
been due to the law of gravity, that law of Nature that mak
unsupported objects, such as apples or stones, fall to the grour
The round arch, as we have seen, was invented in order

---

[1] These pairs of curved timbers were called ' crooks ' and medie
building contracts often specify that a house shall be ' of so many crooks
the corresponding term for the space between pairs of beams is ' bay '.

Barrel Vault

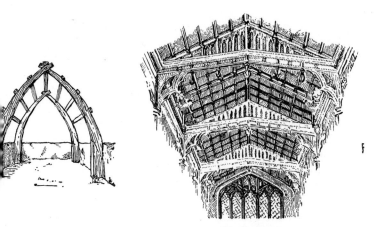

Crooks

Wooden Roof

Vaulting

transfer weight (which is nothing but the pull of gravity) on solid walls or pillars (which are practically isolated pieces wall). These round arches were used by the Saxons and by the Normans for a hundred years after the Conquest. Experimen in the construction of stone vaults proved that instead of makin one long, continuous barrel-vault, it was better to divide the space (whether a room, house, or church) into square section ' bays ', with a support, which might be either a pillar or a wall bracket, at each corner, and carry arches across not only fro side to side but also diagonally from corner to corner, a ' boss or large block of stone being placed at the point where the diagonal arches cross one another. It was also found that fo this purpose round arches were not so good as arches whic were carried up higher in the centre ; in fact the pointed arc was found to be stronger and better for all purposes, and rapidl replaced the round arch ; so that by the end of the twelft century the pointed style of architecture which we call ' Gothic had taken the place of the round style, called ' Romanesque from its having been used in Roman times. By the skilful us of this improved type of arch the weight of the building wa distributed to a limited number of points along the walls, an it was therefore possible to build thinner walls, strengthenir them at these points with buttresses. So we find that Goth buildings are lighter and less massive than Romanesque. Th buttresses also became a decorative feature of these buildings often they are carried up into pinnacles, which are not onl for ornament but by their weight, pressing *downwards*, help t counteract the *outward* pressure of the roof ; sometimes th buttresses are built a little distance away from the walls an only connected with them by stone arches, and these ' flyin buttresses ' add greatly to the beauty of many fine churche such as Westminster Abbey or the French cathedral of Chartre

The reference to Chartres is made because it is important t realize that English architecture was in early days much in fluenced by that of France. The original Abbey church o Westminster, built by Edward the Confessor, was modelled o

he Norman church of Jumièges, and when the Abbey was
rebuilt by Henry III, its design was influenced by that of Rheims
athedral. Even after the loss of Normandy, France and
ngland were closely connected ; French, as we have seen, was
he language of polite society, and as ladies in recent times
ave taken their fashions in hats and clothes from Paris, so the
medieval patrons of art in England took their ideas in archi-
ecture to some extent from France.

he architects were sometimes
renchmen ; but the medieval
rchitect was not a gentleman who
at in his London office and drew
ut elaborate plans with drawings
f every detail, to be carried out
ith mechanical accuracy by un-
intelligent workmen — as is too
ften the case in modern times ;
e was himself a master builder,
ho superintended all the opera-
ions ; his plans were rough, and
he details, especially of decorative
eatures, were largely left to the
ctual workmen, and, as they were

Flying Buttress.

nglishmen, even French designs were given an English flavour.
It is in the carving of the capitals of pillars, of the bosses of
he vaulting, and of the ' corbels ' or stone brackets, that English
eeling is most noticeable, particularly in the quality of humour.
he English workman was always ready for a joke ; the French-
an took his art more seriously and joked with difficulty. The
renchman would carve a gracious saint or grim devil, the
nglishman's saint would very likely be less gracious, his devil
ould be more comic, and often instead of either saint or devil
e would carve a fox preaching to geese, a schoolmaster birching
boy, or a contortionist with his head between his legs. In
erious sculpture on a larger scale, although England was inferior
o France, we can boast of a wonderful series of tombs, of which

the royal tombs at Westminster form the finest group to be seen
in any single church. In particular two schools of English
carvers existed; from the twelfth to the fourteenth century
there was a school of sculptors at Purbeck, in Dorset, who worked
the local marble and carved monumental effigies, of which
numbers remain, such as those of the Knights Templars in the
Temple Church at London. During the fourteenth and fifteenth
centuries an even more remarkable school grew up round Nottingham, where alabaster was worked. The Nottingham carver
worked chiefly on altar-pieces—slabs of alabaster, carved with
sacred subjects, to stand behind an altar; these varied from
a small panel with a conventional representation of the Holy
Trinity, up to great pieces representing scenes from the life of
some saint and containing scores of figures. They were not
only distributed all over England, but were in great demand
on the Continent, and the finest specimens that have survived
are now to be found in France.

England was also famous in the Middle Ages for artistic metal
work, especially in gold and silver, but unfortunately very little
of this has come down to our own times. In one branch of the
art we are able to see that our ancestors were superior to the
craftsmen of other nations. In the Middle Ages legal documents
were sealed, not signed; so everybody of gentle rank owned
a seal, usually of silver or bronze. Many of these still exist, and
of thousands which have disappeared we have impressions in
wax; comparing these with contemporary examples from other
countries, we are able to see not only how beautiful many of
them are, but also how much finer the English work was. The
ironwork on many ancient doors, the locks on old chests and
similar objects also serve to show us that even the village blacksmith had a sense of design and an instinctive love of art.

Although painters were never honoured in medieval England
as they were in Italy, so that we have no record of their lives
and can hardly point to any picture as the work of any particular
artist, their work was in great demand. Practically every church
had its walls covered with paintings; over the chancel arch

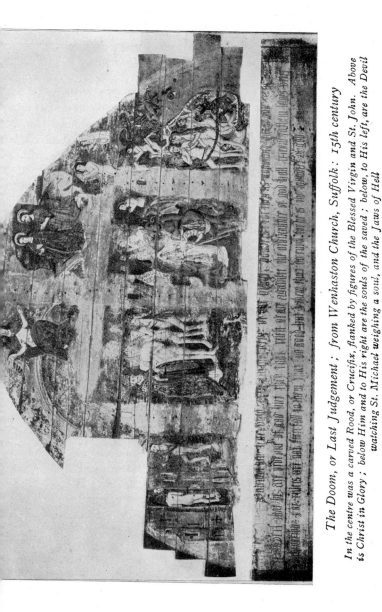

The Doom, or Last Judgement; from Wenhaston Church, Suffolk: 15th century

In the centre was a carved Rood, or Crucifix, flanked by figures of the Blessed Virgin and St. John. Above is Christ in Glory; below Him and to His right are the souls of the saved; below, to His left, are the Devil watching St. Michael weighing a soul, and the Jaws of Hell

M

was usually a picture of the Last Judgement—Christ in glory
in the centre, below him St. Michael is often shown holding
a pair of scales, in one pan of which kneels a little naked soul
while a devil hangs on to the other pan, trying to drag it down
and so get the soul condemned; lower still a crowd of naked
souls rising from their graves, the good being received into
Paradise on the right hand of Christ, the evil being carried off
by grotesque demons to the flames and torments of Hell. On the
other walls were scenes from biblical history or the legends of
the saints or allegorical subjects, such as the Seven Deadly Sins.
Those specimens which have been recovered from the layers of
whitewash with which they were covered by Puritans, who
thought them 'popish' and wicked, and by churchwardens
who thought them ugly, are for the most part interesting rather
than beautiful, but there are a number of examples in Norwich
Cathedral and elsewhere in Norfolk that show that there was an
East Anglian school of painting which might have stood comparison with the Flemish schools if not with those of Italy.
Unluckily the English painters did not often paint movable
pictures on canvas or wooden panels, and hardly any examples
of such work have survived. We can, however, judge the
pictorial ability of medieval Englishmen by their decoration of
manuscripts. Scores of books, from the tenth to the sixteenth
century, most beautifully illustrated, show that in this branch
of art also the English were not inferior to their neighbours.
Before the Conquest the great centre of this art was at Winchester; during the twelfth and thirteenth centuries it was at
York, and later at Canterbury and St. Albans; in the fourteenth
century the East Anglian school produced a number of wonderful
psalters in which the writing is surrounded by borders filled with
quaint and exquisite groups of animals and human figures.
Here, again, the English artists showed their sense of humour
and fun. The margins, even of church service books, are full
of spirited drawings of country dances, children riding hobby
horses or whipping tops, a tournament between knights mounted
on snails, a fox running away with a goose and pursued by a

ld woman with her distaff, hares shooting at dogs, or dressed
n priestly vestments, conducting a funeral service, monkeys at
chool—the schoolmaster monkey beating one of the pupils—

*A MS. of the Winchester school, c. 970 ; representing
the visit of the three kings.*

d so on. The figures, both human and animal, are full of life
d movement, and in one splendid missal painted in Sherborne
bbey is a series of pictures of birds which would put to shame
any modern books of natural history.

In another branch of art, Music, we may also look back upon
r ancestors with respect. In the Middle Ages music was

M 2

a necessary part of a good education ; every knight and lady
was expected at least to be able to join in a song if not to play
some instrument.   Every noble kept a number of minstrels
who played during meal-times and accompanied him on his
journeys, so that the royal court on great occasions must have
been full of musicians if not of melody.   When Edward I kept
Christmas at St. Macaire, in the south of France, in 1287, he
distributed £50 (say £700 of modern money) to 125 musicians
and at the wedding of that king's daughter, Margaret, in 1290
no fewer than 426 minstrels received gifts of money.   The town
also kept their ' waits ', who combined the duties of watchmen
and musicians, and bagpipes seem to have been a necessary part
of a shepherd's equipment.   The instruments used by the
minstrels were varied ; strings, such as the harp, lute, zither
or guitar, several types of violin, and a curious sort of hurdy-
gurdy, played by turning a handle ; wind instruments, such as
trumpets, bagpipes, mouth-organs, and several varieties of
pipes ; also portable organs which were apparently blown with
one hand and played with the other.   Regular organs were
common in churches from Saxon times, and were blown by
hand or by men standing on the bellows : St. Dunstan is said
to have made one with bronze pipes for Malmesbury Abbey
and an ancient writer declares that Bishop Alphage made one
for Winchester Cathedral, in the tenth century, which had
400 pipes and at the blowing of which 70 men laboured till the
sweat poured off them, while its noise could be heard all over
the ancient city of Winchester !

Besides instrumental music, singing was much practised, and
although the English had not that skill in part-singing for which
the Welsh were already famous in the twelfth century, they
were considered a musical race and had a reputation for ' caroles '
or folk-songs in which singing was combined with dancing.
Many of our traditional folk-song tunes descend from these
' caroles ' and from the ballads sung by wandering minstrels.
Apart from their musical ability these minstrels played an
important part in medieval life ; they were to the villager

Musical Instruments of the 14th century

much what newspapers are now ; going freely into the house
of the great and the taverns of the poor, they picked up al
kinds of news and passed it on, often in the form of a ballad
and every great political movement must have been accompanie
by a flood of such rhymes and ballads.

Turning from the Arts to the Sciences, the great differenc
to be observed between medieval and modern science is tha
nowadays every scientific theory is based upon, and tested by
experiments, while in early days there was very little experi
menting, and science was based almost entirely upon tradition
any statement that once got put into writing would be repeate
by author after author, even when a perfectly simple test woul
have shown that it was untrue. The original source of mos
scientific literature was the writings of the great classical author
particularly of Aristotle, and as the Latin translations of hi
works were incomplete and shockingly inaccurate, and th
additions made by commentators were fantastic and wild, th
genuine student was badly handicapped in his search for trutl
Roger Bacon of Oxford, who lived during the reign of Henry II
was the one great original student of science who saw the nece
sity of experiment and of studying the actual works of the grea
writers and not merely other men's comments on their writings
he spent his life and a great fortune on such research, and h
reward was to be cast into prison by the authorities of th
Church, who were too often the enemies of originality in thougl
and learning. Even when writers tried to record facts that the
had themselves observed they were usually inaccurate, thoug
some medical writers, such as John of Gaddesden, a famor
doctor of the fourteenth century, did show considerable powe
of observation. John of Gaddesden may be taken as a typ
of the better medieval scientists ; his work is full of sour
medical advice, part of it derived from ancient Greek and Arabi
authors (through Latin translations), but much of it due to h
own practical experience, yet it is also full of false argumen
and foolishness, such as charms ; his prescriptions often conta
drugs which are still recognized as the correct remedies for t!

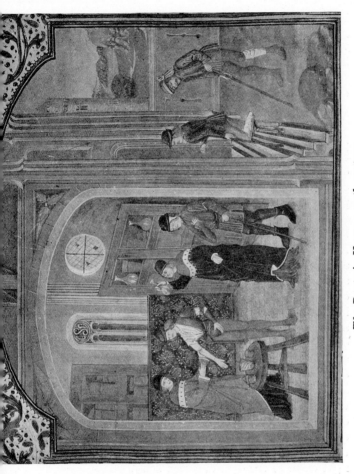

The Doctor's House: 15th century

Arrival and examination of patients

particular diseases treated by him, but often they are mere
jumbles of all kinds of ingredients, of which most were entirely
valueless—medieval medicines often containing twenty or thirty
herbs and mineral substances.

Medical science has never been entirely free from humbug:
even modern doctors have been known to pretend to be wiser
than they are, and one medieval book written for the use of
doctors gives much advice on how to impress a patient and his
friends with your wisdom : for instance, if you do not know what
is the matter, say that the patient is suffering from obstruction
of the liver : ' Be sure to use the word " obstruction ", for they
don't understand it, and it is often exceedingly useful that
people should not understand what you say.'   Besides this
deliberate humbug there was a good deal that would be called
by that name now, but was intended seriously at the time.
Reference has already been made to charms, and on much the
same level were the mystic properties ascribed to various precious
stones, the wearing of which was supposed to prevent or cure
certain diseases.   The sapphire in particular was believed to
have curative powers ; as an instance of this belief we find
a man in 1391 leaving a ring with a sapphire to the priest of the
chantry of St. James at Scarborough, ' so that it may be available for all who desire the medical aid of the said ring '.   Another
curious belief was that scrofula, a skin disease popularly known
as ' the king's evil ', could be cured by the touch of the king—
this miraculous gift of healing being said to have been granted
divinely to Edward the Confessor and his successors ; consequently we find Edward I ' touching ' batches of as many as
two hundred sufferers at one time, and the practice continued
right down to the days of Queen Anne.

Astronomy, a science almost entirely derived from the great
Arabian scientists and mathematicians—or rather that branch
of astronomy known as astrology—was a necessary part of
a medieval doctor's studies.   By astrology he could tell from the
position of the stars whether a patient was likely to recover,
and by the phases of the moon and stars he would decide whether

or not to bleed a patient, and if so from which veins to draw the blood. Nor was astrology only of use in medicine; the same science could be used to discover the whereabouts of stolen property and the identity of the thief. Another magical method of detecting thieves was by crystal-gazing; in this the magician, or a child employed by him, gazed into a crystal ball or on the bright blade of a sword until he saw in it a picture of the thief or of the place where the goods were hidden. Such magic might be harmless enough, except that it often led to false accusations against innocent people, but there were other kinds of magical science which were intended to be harmful. It is very difficult to say how much truth there was in the medieval superstition of witchcraft; but there certainly were persons—usually old women—who were believed, and believed themselves, to have the power of causing their enemies to fall ill and even to die. Whatever view we may take of magic and witchcraft, it is important to remember that people in the Middle Ages firmly believed in them and in the constant presence of the Devil and his wicked spirits in their midst. Perfectly natural events were therefore often attributed to supernatural causes, and scientists who indulged in experimental research were suspected of witchcraft and other sinful acts; all of which tended to discourage such research and to hinder the proper study of science.

IX

WARFARE

WAR in the Middle Ages was not an exceptional and disturbin
occurrence, but part of the normal conditions of life. It was th
profession of the upper classes, and the divisions of medieva
society were based almost as much on the practice of war as o
the possession of land. The combination of the two, the holdin
of land by military tenure, constituted the Feudal System
introduced into England by the Normans.

Under the Saxons every holder of land had to assist in keepin
up the *burhs* or fortified townships, and every free man had t
follow his lord to battle, but the obligation was a personal on
and was not connected with the land ; because one holder of a
estate followed a particular noble it was not necessary that th
next holder of that estate should attach himself to the same noble
The nobles, or thanes, also had to come fully armed to serve th
king, and apparently to provide a certain number of arme
soldiers ; but although the possession of five hides of land wa
one of the qualifications for the rank of thane, such military
service was not the condition on which the land was held. O
the Continent there had grown up a system by which the emperor
and kings granted large portions of their realms to nobles wh
in return took oaths of ' fealty ', or faithfulness, and undertoo
to assist their royal master with a certain number of armed me
in time of war. In order to secure the services of these arme
men, the great nobles in turn granted portions of their lands t
men who swore fealty to them and promised to fight for thei
lords when required. And as the land was given expressly o
this condition of military service, it followed that even if th
original grantee parted with it the new tenant would be boun
to serve. The service demanded was that of a fully arme
horseman, or knight, and the estate which had to provide one

A Battle Scene
15th century

such knight was called a ' knight's fee '. (Great estates are usuall
called ' fiefs ' ; in each case the Latin word is *feodum* or *feudun*
whence our adjective ' feudal '.) In this way each great lor
could raise a force of cavalry by simply sending a summons t
his tenants, which made it easy for the king to collect an army—
provided his great lords remained faithful, but if they rebelle
this system placed a powerful weapon in their hands.

When William of Normandy conquered England he distribute
the land among his followers and friends to be held on thi
system of military tenure, each group of estates (or manors
being bound to provide a particular number of knights. Th
estates, as we have seen, were assessed for purposes of taxatio
in hides, but the number of knights demanded did not depen
on the number of hides (except that at least five hides wer
allowed for each knight's fee) or upon anything except the wil
of the Conqueror. If he chose to give one man 400 hides in returr
for the service of two knights, while he demanded from anothe
thirty knights for 200 hides, he did so and there was no more t
be said about it. Such was the estate and such was the service
and if the owner of the lordship did not produce his knights when
required his land would be seized. The total number of knights
fees thus created in England seems to have been between six
and seven thousand. Nor did William trouble about how the
knights were to be provided ; that was the affair of the lords. As
a rule they secured them by granting portions of their lands to
lesser men to hold on similar terms ; and this process of ' sub-
infeudation ' might be carried further, so that A would hold of
the king by the service of twenty knights, B would hold of A
by the service of four knights, and C hold a knight's fee of B.
If A, the tenant-in-chief, who held directly of the king, did not
' enfeoff ' (i.e. grant fees to) all the knights that he owed, the
remainder were charged on ' the demesne ', that is to say the
estates which remained in his own hands, and these estates
might be seized for any deficiency. Sometimes a tenant-in-chief
would enfeoff more knights than he actually owed. This gave
him a margin in case any one defaulted, and had other advantages;

r on the death of a military tenant his heir had to pay a certain
ım as ' relief ' (or death duties) to his immediate overlord, and
the heir were under age the overlord had the custody of his
nds until he came of age, which was often a source of consider-
ble profit. Normandy itself was a fief of France, and the Dukes
f Normandy, thanks to the number of their military tenants,
ad often proved thorns in the side of the kings of France.

Making a Knight: c. 1250.
The king girds on his sword, while attendants fasten on his spurs.

William did not intend that this state of affairs should be repeated to his own disadvantage, and, therefore, caused all the
ubtenants as well as the tenants-in-chief to swear fealty to him,
hereby bringing them more directly under his own influence.

Knighthood, then, was in practice the liability to serve in the
cavalry in return for the possession of land ; and from the
thirteenth century onwards it became the custom to force all
persons who held lands above a certain value (usually fixed at
£20 a year—say, £350 of modern money) to become knights,
under penalty of a fine. But knighthood was also an honour and
made the recipient a member of the lesser nobility. There was,

indeed, in early times no strict line between the knights and th
barons, or peers ; the distinction was a matter of tenure—
a tenant-in-chief held his lands ' by barony ' he paid on succeedin
to his estates a fixed ' relief ' of £100, whereas a knight paid £
for each fee that he held. The knight was created by the kin
or by some great lord by the ceremony of girding him wit
a sword, and in token of the high ideals which were supposed t
inspire him, this sword lay during the night before the ceremon
upon the altar in the church, and there the candidate for knight
hood kept his vigil. Similarly the ceremonial bath which gav
its name to the Order of the Bath, founded in 1399, was a symbo
of the purity and clean life expected of the aspirant to knighthood
There were also the definitely religious Orders of the Temple an
of the Hospital of St. John of Jerusalem, both founded in con
nexion with the Crusades. The Knights Templars and th
Hospitallers alike were warriors who took semi-monastic vow
and lived in communities apart. The Templars fought heroicall
in Palestine, but by their pride and wealth made enemies, wh
accused them of heresy and the practice of magic, learnt from
their Saracen enemies, and the Pope caused the suppression o
the Order in 1312, which was carried out with much cruelty or
the Continent, but with comparative mildness in England.

The downfall of the Templars, thus charged with betrayin
the Faith which their Order was founded to defend, may serve
to remind us of the difference between the theory and practice
of knighthood. The ideal of the knight, as stated by an English
writer in the twelfth century, was : ' to protect the Church, tc
fight against treachery, to reverence the priesthood, to defend
the poor from injustice, to make peace in his own province, tc
shed his blood for his brethren, and, if necessary, to lay down his
life '. Such ideals Chaucer's ' very perfit gentil knight ' kept
before his eyes, and such a knight we find in real life in the person
of Sir Robert Umfraville, Warden of the Northern Marches, as
described by one who knew and served him. Sir Robert, a
Knight of the Garter, was a man of clean life, wise, cheerful and
courtly, of unblemished honour ; a lion in battle, but so just

hat even his Scottish enemies sought his decisions rather than
those of their own judges ; comparatively poor, but generous,
nd so kindly that he would not even shame his servants by
reproving them for their misdeeds in the presence of their fellows.
uch men have been rare at all times, and Piers Plowman asked
o more of his typical knight than that he should defend the
Church, hunt the birds and beasts that damage poor men's
rops, and refrain from oppressing his tenants. Even this was
, higher standard than most attained ; they were knights who
lew Thomas Becket, Archbishop of Canterbury, before the altar ;
nights, like Sir John de Warenne, forbade their tenants to drive
he deer and other game out of their cornfields ; and few knights
howed much consideration for the poor. Chivalry, indeed, was
, class conception, an elaborate and ornate code of courtesy
owards equals and superiors, which concerned itself little with
he existence of inferiors.

War is at best a brutal business, bringing out the worst side of
uman nature. It also calls for courage and endurance and lends
tself to picturesque acts of valour, which stand out all the
righter against the black background, so that we are apt to
verlook the beastliness in admiration of the heroic. This is
particularly the case with medieval warfare ; there is a glamour
about swords and spears and arrows and glittering armour, which
is absent from rifles, trench mortars and bombs ; writers have
naturally preferred to dwell upon the more romantic incidents
of battles, and there is a general impression that war in the
Middle Ages was, in comparison with modern war, gentle and
humane. It was not. It is true that for a great man, whose
costly armour would make him almost invulnerable, while his
wealth would ensure his good treatment if captured, war had less
terrors in early times than in these days of undiscriminating
bullets, but for the ordinary person war has always been much
the same. The idea that ' frightfulness '—the policy of inflicting
savage punishments for slight offences in order to strike terror
into the hearts of possible enemies—was a new invention of the
late European War is still farther from the truth. Cruelty,

organized and casual, always has been inseparable from war
The worst crimes committed in Flanders during the recent wa
were almost insignificant compared with the cruelties of the
Spaniards in the same district in the sixteenth century. In 1418
a chronicler records that the English troops took Pontoise with
out any resistance, ' where, according to the usual custom in
conquered towns, they committed innumerable injuries ' ; some
forty years earlier, when Rheims refused to send supplies to the
English army, the troops burnt sixty villages in the neighbourhood and informed the townsmen that they would burn all the
standing corn if they did not send bread and wine at once.
About the same time the Black Prince, justly renowned for his
chivalry, suppressed a rebellion in Limoges, where, in the words
of a contemporary :

'It was great pity to see the men, women, and children, that
kneeled down on their knees before the Prince for mercy ; but
he was so inflamed with ire that he took no heed to them, so
that none was heard, but all put to death as they were met with,
and such as were nothing culpable. There was no pity taken of
the poor people who wrought never no manner of treason, yet
they bought it dearer than the great. There was not so hard
a heart within the city of Limoges, if he had any remembrance
of God, but wept piteously for the great mischief that they saw
before their eyes ; for more than three thousand men, women,
and children were slain and beheaded that day. God have mercy
on their souls, for I trowe they were martyrs.'

Still earlier, Edward I, a stern but by no means savage king, was
so angered by the insults of the men of Berwick that he ordered
the massacre of the entire population of the town and was with
difficulty turned from his purpose by the prayers of the clergy.
William the Conqueror so ravaged the rebellious province of
Yorkshire that the inhabitants were reduced to starvation, even
to cannibalism, and tracts of country were still desolate twenty
years later. When such things were done by disciplined armies
under leaders of more than average humanity, it may well be
believed that the deeds of the savage Scots and Irish and of the
lawless barons of Stephen's feeble reign will not bear description.

Soldiers pillaging a house: 15th century

Archers: c. 1340

Even when such savagery was not part of the policy of th
commander, it must have been very difficult to maintain disciplir
in a medieval army. The regulations for the army of Henry V-
that army whose conduct in the neighbourhood of Rheims w
have just noticed—were excellent, prohibiting the robbery o
churches, violence towards women, the capture of children, th
plundering of peasants, or the destruction of crops and fru
trees, and similar offences, and Henry made some attempt t
enforce them but, it would seem, with little success. In earlie
times it must have been still more difficult owing to the way i
which medieval armies were raised.

The Saxons fought always on foot, though they frequentl
rode to the field of battle ; their weapons were the sword, ax
and spear ; of defensive armour few except the thanes—who ha
helm and hauberk, or coat of mail—had more than a leather
cap and a shield, which was round in early times but was kit
shaped in the eleventh century. The thanes probably had t
attend the king in time of war as his bodyguard and as office
over the other troops. There was an arrangement by whic
every five hides of land had to provide one fully armed soldie
and in addition every able-bodied man was liable to serve in th
fyrd or militia. In actual practice the *fyrd* was only called u
from the district threatened by the enemy. These men wer
armed with whatever weapons they could get, spears, flail
clubs, slings, and a small type of bow, and served as a usefu
backing to the better armed troops, but had probably little ide
of discipline. Brave enough in battle, they were not easy to kee
together for prolonged operations ; Harold's southern *fyrd*, afte
waiting some time for William's expected expedition fro
Normandy, had to be allowed to go home to get in the harves
so that his landing at Pevensey was unopposed.

Although the *fyrd* was called out by William Rufus and at th
beginning of the reign of Henry I, the Norman Conquest brough
a complete change in military matters. The Normans depende
almost entirely upon their cavalry, such infantry as they ha
being mainly archers—still armed with the small bow, which wa

rawn only to the breast. The Norman knight wore a conical
ap strengthened with cross-pieces of iron, a long coat of mail—
ormed by sewing rings or small plates of metal on to the leather
f the coat—and carried a large kite-shaped shield, a pennoned
nce and a heavy sword, or sometimes a mace, or iron club. We
ave already seen how, by the distribution of knight's fees,
 supply of knights was secured; such knights were bound to
rve at their own expense for forty days, at the end of which
riod, if they continued in the army, they were entitled to
ages. An army so raised would obviously consist of a large
umber of dissimilar detachments, one baron bringing perhaps
 hundred knights, another only two or three; the difficulty
f brigading such varying detachments and persuading them to
ct together must have been great. Moreover, if operations
sted beyond the forty days, a certain number of the knights
ould probably insist upon returning home. So, early in the
velfth century, was introduced the system of ' scutage ' (Latin
utum = a shield = an armed man) by which a baron might pay
 fixed sum (usually 40s., the equivalent of forty days' wages)
stead of bringing a knight, and might raise that sum from the
night who would otherwise have had to serve in person; with
e money so obtained the king could hire knights, or men-at-
rms, who being mercenaries, professional soldiers, would be
ore under control.

For the reorganization of the national forces an ' Assize of
rms ' was issued in 1181, by which every holder of a knight's
e or of property worth £10 was to keep a coat of mail, a helmet,
 shield, and a lance; the owner of property worth £6 should
ave a ' hauberk ' (a light coat of mail), an iron headpiece, and
 lance, and all free men should have a ' wambais ' (a quilted
cket, stuffed with wool and more or less sword-proof), iron
eadpiece and lance. By a revision of the Assize thirty years
ter the owner of property worth twenty shillings had to keep
 bow and arrows. These arms were never to be parted with, but
anded down from father to son. The Assize was repeated, with
ight alterations, in the Statute of Winchester in 1285, showing

that the obligation of all men to serve if called upon was st
recognized ; but in practice no such universal levy was ev
made at that period.

The great period of army reform was the reign of Edward
That king was the greatest soldier of his day, and it was large
owing to the changes made by him that the English army becam
the formidable force which it proved to be during the Hundr
Years' War. The heavy cavalry—who were armed from head
foot in chain-mail (mail in which the rings, instead of being sev
separately on to the leather coat, were interlaced) with weigh
pot-helms, small shields and heavy lances and swords, and ro
powerful chargers protected with armour—continued to be t
picked troops ; but Edward's experience in Palestine and Wal
led him to introduce light cavalry, less heavily armed an
mounted on swifter, unprotected, horses. Much more importa
than this was his introduction of the long-bow. At the beginni
of his reign the archers were almost entirely cross-bowmen an
mostly foreign mercenaries. The cross-bow, shooting a heav
bolt, was a powerful instrument in the hands of experts ; it wa
indeed, so deadly that when first introduced in the twelfth centu
it was denounced by the Church as an unchristian and inhuma
weapon. As, however, war is not often successfully conduct
on Christian and humane lines, these denunciations were no mo
effective than the outcry against submarines and poison-gas
recent times. The chief drawback to the cross-bow was that
could not be loaded rapidly ; the ordinary bow, on the oth
hand, could be fired with great rapidity, and it had by this tin
developed—not yet into the six-foot bow of Robin Hood, b
into a real long-bow, drawn to the ear and not only to the breas
which gave it far greater force and accuracy. In his Wel
campaigns Edward introduced the practice of brigading arche
with his cavalry, placing them on the flanks and between t
squadrons. This manœuvre, combined with the skill attain
by the English bowmen, who could shoot with accuracy to
range of over 200 yards, was mainly responsible for the brillia
victories of the Hundred Years' War, such as Crécy. Not on

as the arrow a deadly weapon, piercing chain-mail, but the
[ef]fect of a hail of arrows is said by those who have experienced
[it] to be far more confusing than that of a hail of bullets. The
[en]emy's cavalry, trying to avoid the storm of arrows, tended to
[h]uddle together and charge blindly on to the English lances,
[ex]posing their flanks to the archers as they did so.

The great feature in the tactics of the native English army
[h]ad been the shield-wall ; the entire force was drawn up in a mass,

The Shield-wall at the Battle of Hastings.

[th]e front line being occupied by the fully armed troops with their
[s]hields touching and forming a wall of defence for the archers,
[sl]ingers, and light-armed men. Where the flanks were protected
[b]y natural features such a formation had great power of resistance,
[a]s was shown at the battles of Stamford Bridge and Hastings
[in] 1066 and at the Battle of the Standard in 1138, which was
[p]robably the last important instance of its employment. Then,
[a]s we have just seen, came the period of cavalry fighting, followed
[b]y combined cavalry and archers. The next step was a return
[t]o the English custom of fighting on foot. The value of dis-
[m]ounted cavalry was shown in 1322 at Boroughbridge and again

a few years later in Scotland at Duplin Moor, and was repeated
demonstrated in the wars with France. The French continue
to despise their infantry and rely upon their knightly cavalr
for which they paid a heavy penalty at Agincourt. Englan
relied more and more upon her archers and pikemen, until,
the middle of the fifteenth century a London chronicler cou'
record sarcastically: ' as for spearmen, they be good to ri
before the footmen and eat and drink up their victual, and man
more such pretty things they do, . . . for in the footmen is a
the trust.'

The infantry were raised, after the twelfth century, by
modification of the *fyrd* system. In time of war orders were se
to the sheriffs of counties near the part of England concerned,
provide a definite number of men. For a Scottish expediti
the men were drawn from the northern counties, for war wit
France from the southern, against Wales from the wester.
The full number demanded was rarely, if ever, reached, and th
quality of the troops left much to be desired, as the recruitir
officers often took bribes to excuse suitable men and accepte
unfit and worthless substitutes. Shakespeare's inimitab
description of Falstaff raising his troop of scarecrows, an
incidentally lining his purse at the same time, though draw
from his Elizabethan contemporaries seems to have been tri
for earlier times as well. Of those raked in, many deserted befo
they reached head-quarters, and there was a continual leaka
during the war, especially when, as was usually the case, the
pay was in arrears. To swell their numbers tramps and sturc
beggars were pressed into the service, and the prisons we
emptied into the army—Edward I in one single year pardoni
450 murderers besides lesser offenders. It is not altogeth
surprising that armies so recruited should have committe
atrocities, and that the disbanded troops after a campaign we
a nuisance and a danger to their fellow-countrymen. But th
fought all right.

These levies were arranged in groups of twenty men wit
a ' vintenar ' at their head, and were further grouped in hundre

nd thousands under mounted officers. A medieval army
arely exceeded 10,000 men, the proportion of cavalry and infantry
arying. There was no regular uniform, though occasionally
town or county would equip its detachment in some particular
olour—as, for instance,
he 'Blaunchecotes'
white coats) raised in
Norfolk for one of the
ampaigns of Edward I
—and in the fifteenth
century all the English
nfantry in France wore
vhite armlets with the
ed cross of St. George.
The retainers of the great
ords also would wear
a livery (French *livrée* =
apparel *presented* to the
wearer) of their lord's
colours and marked with
his badge. The lords and
knights themselves were
distinguished by their
armorial bearings.

Heraldry, the science
of armorial bearings,
came into prominence
with the appearance of
a type of helm which con-

Garter Stall-plate of Sir Ralph Bassett :
c. 1370.

cealed much of the face, in the twelfth century. It was impossible
in the confusion of a battle to tell whether a knight was your
friend, Sir Ralph Homard, or your enemy, Sir Bertram Poulet; the
only course was to label the knight. The broad, smooth surface
of the shield was the obvious place for a label; a name would
not be easily distinguished, especially by persons who could not
read, so, just as shops and inns were marked by painted signs, it

became the custom to decorate the shields with simple device
in bright colours. These devices were combinations of broa
bands of colour or conventional representations of beasts an
birds—lions and eagles being naturally favourite subjects—o
of other objects. Very often the objects had some punnin
allusion to the bearer's name ; thus Trumpington bore tw
trumpets, Picot three picks, Alcock cocks' heads, Erneley ' ernes
(an old word for eagles), Lucy ' luces ' (the fish now called pike
Martell hammers (French *martel*), Malbysse hinds' heads (Frenc
biche), Butler cups, and so on. Individuals, no doubt, painte
devices on their shields as early as the Conquest, but it was onl
in the latter part of the twelfth century that the practice becam
common and that the devices became recognized as the mark
of particular families and were handed on from father to son
Any man of respectable position might assume such arms as h
chose, provided that they had not already been assumed b
any one else, and they would then become the property of hi
descendants. The Crusades, bringing together so many knight
who were unknown to each other, gave an impetus to the practic
of wearing arms, and the introduction of the surcoat—or line
garment worn over the armour, partly to lessen the violence o
the eastern sun—led to the arms being embroidered upon i
(whence our expression ' a coat of arms '). They were als
embroidered upon the trappings of the horses and on the flag
of the knights. Every knight had the right to use a pennon o
small flag with a forked tail ; if he distinguished himself i
battle he was raised to the rank of a knight banneret, and hi
pennon was converted into a square banner by cutting off the tail

Besides the arms thus displayed, a device was often worn o
the helmet, particularly at tournaments and in processions ; thi
was the ' crest '. It was often of great size, but did not add mucl
to the weight of the helm, as it was hollow and constructed of ligh
materials. At the point where the crest joined the helm the latte
was encircled by a twisted scarf of two colours, forming th
' wreath ' (represented in modern heraldry by the thing lik
a bit of barley-sugar underneath a crest) and hanging down to

orm the ' mantling '. Finally there was the ' badge ', a device which was not usually hereditary, but belonged to a particular person and was used by his household. Familiar badges are the ostrich feathers of the Prince of Wales, the red and white roses of Lancaster and York, and the combined rose of the Tudors, the white hart of Richard II, the swan of Henry IV, the boar of Richard III, the portcullis of Henry VII, which appears so frequently on his chapel at Westminster Abbey.

Heraldry added much to the splendour and picturesqueness of me-dieval life. The strong contrasting colours and bold designs possessed a decorative value which appealed to a race who had an appreciation of colour and line which has been lost in modern times. Armorial bear-ings soon passed beyond their original limits of flags and armour ; they

Seal of Richard Neville, Earl of Warwick.

figured on the seals for which the English engravers were so justly famous ; they blazed in the stained glass of churches and palaces ; they were carved and painted on tombs ; lords and ladies wore splendid heraldic robes and mantles, hung their halls with heraldic tapestries and slept in beds that were gorgeous with heraldic embroideries. Moreover, the history of the Middle Ages is written in heraldry. The addition of the fleurs-de-lys of France to the leopards of England in the royal arms marks the claim of Ed-ward III to the crown of France, which formed the pretext for the Hundred Years' War, as, at a later date, the addition of the arms of Scotland marks the accession of the Stuart line. The wounded Scottish lion on the shield of the Dukes of Norfolk tells of the fatal field of Flodden, where the English under a Duke of Norfolk crushed the army of Scotland ; and the group of arms on the shield of Richard, Earl of Warwick, tells how the titles, lands and wealth of Nevill, Beauchamp, Montague, Monthermer, and Despenser had come, by marriage and descent, to him and help to explain how he came to be ' the king-maker ' and foremost figure of his day.

As the possession of a coat of arms was the mark of a gentle man, so skill in war and the use of weapons was the great object of his education. John Hardyng, who was himself as a boy in the household of the famous Sir Henry Percy (Hotspur), tells us that lords' sons were set at four years old to learn their letters at six to learn grammar and table manners and courtesy ; at fourteen they were taken hunting, to give them courage and self-reliance ; and at sixteen they were ready to take the field in tournaments or war, practising daily deeds of arms. To give young knights practice and their elders excitement tournaments or jousts were held. These seem to have sprung up in France in the twelfth century and were popular with the Anglo-Norman knights ; the sons of Henry II often attended them, and William the Marshal, afterwards Earl of Pembroke and regent of England during the minority of Henry III, was the most brilliant jouster of his day. These early tournaments were very rough affairs, in every sense, quite unlike the chivalrous contests of later days ; the rival parties fought in groups, and it was considered not only fair but commendable to hold off until you saw some of your adversaries getting tired and then to join the attack on them ; the object was not to break a lance in the most approved style but frankly to disable as many opponents as possible for the sake of obtaining their horses, arms, and ransoms. The Marshal, who started life as a penniless younger son, made a very good income out of his tournaments. Popes and popular preachers vainly denounced the practice ; tournaments continued to be held, and Edward I in particular was their great patron. As time went on, however, they became more orderly and developed into the chivalrous encounters dear to writers of romances. In the ' jousts

A Tournament: c. 1475

The Earl of Warwick is distinguished by his crest of the Bear and Ragged
Staff, and his page has the Earl's badge of the Ragged Staff on his back. On
the left the Judges are examining tilting lances.

of peace ' of the fifteenth century there was much picturesque
ceremony and a great display of splendour ; the tilting ground
was crowded with onlookers, and the grand stand was full of
lords and ladies in their most magnificent costumes ; the com-
batants were gorgeously or fantastically arrayed ; they used
lances with blunt points and charged down opposite sides of
a barrier, which prevented their horses colliding ; the object of
each was to unhorse or unhelm his opponent or to break his own
spear by a fair and square blow on the other's shield or helm ;
six or eight courses would be run by each pair of knights, and
umpires kept the score on a regular system of points and dis-
qualified any competitor who struck his opponent's horse or
inflicted any other foul blow ; at the end of the day the winner
was presented with a prize by the queen of the tourney.

Armour had changed greatly between the time of the Norman
Conquest and the days of these tournaments. The coat of mail
had given way to the complete suit of closely fitting mail, made
of interwoven rings. Next, in the thirteenth century, extra
protection was given to the knee-caps and elbows by plates of
metal and to the neck by plates (' aillettes ') standing up from
the shoulders to break a sweeping sword stroke. About the same
time came in the pot-helm, not unlike a handleless saucepan,
which came down on to the shoulders, having slits in front for
the wearer to see and breathe through. Another form of headpiece in use, with slight variations, through most part of the
Middle Ages, was the ' basnet ', a conical steel cap with a ' gorget '
or neck-piece either of mail or of plate, and a movable ' visor ',
pierced with holes, which could be pulled down to cover the face.
Additional protection was gradually afforded to vulnerable parts
by plates of metal, until by the middle of the fifteenth century
the knight was clad completely in plate armour, the mail sur-
viving only as a protection to the joints of the plates. A knight
arming for a tournament would first put on a padded doublet of
cloth, lined with satin, a pair of trunk-hose of stout cloth and
a pair of stout shoes. On the doublet would be sewn diamond-
shaped gussets of mail over the armpits and elbow-joints, and on

A Mêlée, c. 1400

A Mêlée, c. 1425

the hose similar gussets under the knees and over the insteps. The first piece of armour put on would be (1) the ' Sabatynes ' or over-shoes of plate ; then (2) the ' Greaves ' would be buckled on to the legs, followed by (3) the ' Cuisses ' or thigh-pieces, with knee-plates attached. Next (4) the ' Breech ' or petticoat of mail was tied round the waist, covering the top of the cuisses. Then the main piece of body armour (5), the Breast-plate, which included the Back-plate, as the two were buckled together and formed one whole, to which were fastened (6) the ' Tuilettes '— ' little tiles ' or overlapping plates. After this came (7) the 'Vambrace' (French *avant-bras*), from wrist to elbow, and (8) the ' Rerebrace ' or ' Brassart ', from elbow to shoulder. The inside of the right arm was often protected by a long plate (the ' Moton ') screwed on to the breast-plate ; the left arm being covered by the shield did not require such extra protection. The hands were encased in (9) ' Gauntlets '. On his head would be (10) a ' Basnet ', fastened on to breast- and back-plates by buckles or staples ; in war the basnet would have a visor, but for a tournament no visor would be worn, but the basnet would be covered by a great tilting-helm with crest and mantling. The knight would wear his sword in its sheath on his left side and a dagger on his right, and his shield hanging by a strap round his neck on his left side. Over his armour he might wear a ' Jupon ', or short surcoat, of linen or silk embroidered with his arms. His spear and tilting helm would be carried, until the time came for him to use them, by an attendant squire or page.

These orderly tournaments, in which serious injuries were uncommon, were no doubt an improvement upon the earlier rough-and-tumble contests, in which fatal accidents (if they can be called accidents) were frequent, but they serve to emphasize the point we have already made, that by the fifteenth century the age of the knight as the great fighting man was over. Knights might continue to flatter themselves that cavalry were the really important part of the army, but shrewd business men could see that ' in the footmen is all the trust '. And one thing that was hastening the downfall of the knights was the growing use of gunpowder, which was beginning to make defensive armour useless. Gunpowder had been introduced into England early in the reign of Edward III, and there were a few cannon employed at the battle of Crécy, though they seem to have created more impression by their noise and novelty than by any damage that they wrought. The early cannon were almost all breech-loaders, consisting of two parts—a barrel, strengthened by a number of iron rings, and a ' chamber ', or short cylinder in which the charge of gunpowder was put and which was then fastened into the base of the barrel. There were also ' bombards ', or mortars—short, fat, muzzle-loading pieces—which fired balls of as much as 18 inches diameter and 225 lb. weight. Their range was short and any accuracy of aim must have been practically impossible, as the mounting was very rough ; heavy siege-pieces were often simply fastened on to massive planks—in which case elevation was obtained by driving wedges under the front of the plank. The balls were at first made of stone, like those used from Roman times down to the fifteenth century in the great catapults or ' balistae ', but later they were usually of iron. There were various types of hand-guns in use during the later Middle Ages, mostly miniature cannons mounted on long wooden stocks which were held under the arm or against the shoulder or, when carried by horsemen, against the breast-plate. In battles these hand-guns, against which armour was useless, were more effective than the cannon, but it was the immense superiority of cannon over any other form of siege artillery that made the introduction of gunpowder so important. Castles lost much of their military value, and the fact that the Crown had a practical monopoly of mobile artillery was one of the reasons why the Tudor monarchs were able to put down rebellions so successfully.

Castles had been introduced into England by the Normans. The favourite type at the time of the Conquest was the motte-and-bailey ; in this type the chief defence was a tower erected on the top of an artificial mound, or ' motte '. As it is impossible to place a heavy weight of masonry on such a mound until the earth has had some years to settle down and become solid, the towers were always of timber at first, but were usually replaced in course of time by a wall of stone running round the top of the motte and known as a ' shell-keep '. The bailey, or court, attached to the motte was surrounded by a bank and outer ditch, the bank being strengthened with a stockade ; the gatehouse was probably in many cases built of stone. In some castles, as, for instance, the Tower of London, instead of a motte a great square tower was built on the solid ground. As a rule, in these towers or ' keeps ' the entrance was on the first floor at a considerable height from the ground by means of a drawbridge. During the twelfth century many stone castles were built, Henry II spending great sums on such fortresses as Dover, Oxford, Nottingham, and Scarborough, but the great period of military architecture was the reign of Edward I, by whom were built the magnificent Welsh castles—such as Conway, Carnarvon, and Harlech—in which military strength is combined with beauty of design. In castles of this period the main features may be given briefly as, a broad ditch or moat, usually full of water, surrounding the whole site ; a massive wall rising from the ditch and pierced with occasional slits for archers to shoot through ; towers at intervals, especially at the angles of the walls, projecting so that the garrison could shoot at any one at the foot of the wall. A walk ran along the inner side of the top of the wall, protected by a parapet and battlements, of which the open spaces were originally often closed with shutters or with sloping wooden screens, under which the archers could shoot without exposing themselves ; the towers had conical roofs and often carried projecting wooden galleries. The gatehouse was approached by a drawbridge across the moat ; when this bridge was raised it not only prevented access but formed a protective covering to the gate. The entrance was closed by massive wooden gates and by at least one portcullis, a great frame of bars crossing at right angles, like a harrow, which ran in grooves on either side of the entrance and could be raised by means of counterpoise weights, like a sash window. The parapet of the gatehouse was carried out on stone brackets between which were spaces, ' machicolations ',

Attack on a Castle: c. 1460

A Bombard, or Mortar, and Cannon are shown in action

through which stones, boiling water, burning pitch, and oth
unpleasant substances could be dropped on enemies trying
break down the gates. Against the inner side of the wa
would be the guardrooms, soldiers' quarters, storehouses, stable
and so forth; in the great court would be the hall and chap
and other buildings, and at one point would be the keep or stron
hold of the castle, which could be defended even if the rest of th
place were captured. Such a building might well withstand th
armies of a kingdom before the coming of gunpowder, but heav
artillery soon made the medieval castle a trap for its garriso
rather than a defence, and the military architects of the sixteen
century had to cope with the problem of defence against cann
by the less picturesque but more effective device of earthwork

To write of English warfare without mentioning the nav
would be absurd, though not so absurd when dealing with th
Middle Ages as it would be for any later period. The first pers
to grasp the importance of sea-power for Britain may be said
have been the Belgian adventurer, Carausius, who in A.D. 28
being in command of the Roman fleet in the Channel, proclaim
himself Emperor and succeeded in retaining the title until
was murdered eight years later. Just six hundred years lat
Alfred the Great began the policy of the big battleship b
building a number of great vessels, twice as large as those of th
Danish pirates; it is true that they proved unwieldy and n
very effective, but Alfred deserves praise for seeing that the pla
to meet a foreign enemy was on the sea, and for building somethi
in the nature of a national navy. Just about another six hundr
years passed before a serious attempt was again made to foun
a navy; this time so successfully that it became and has remain
the chief defence of England. During the period between th
reigns of Alfred and Henry VII the nation possessed no regul
force of fighting-ships. As men were called from the ploug
and the loom to fight in the *fyrd*, so the ships of the fisherm
and merchants were formed into fleets. And as there was a lar
body of men who held by military tenure and formed the bac
bone of the early medieval army, so there was a small group

aports that owed naval service to the Crown and formed the
ckbone of the early navy. This group was the Cinque Ports.

The federation of the Five Ports, or Cinque Ports as they are
ually called, already existed at the time of the Conquest and
ossibly owed its origin to Earl Godwin. The head of the
leration was Hastings, the other ports being Dover, Sandwich,
ythe, and Romney, to which were added at an early date the

ncient towns' of Rye
d Winchelsea. The
iginal bond of union
tween these Sussex and
entish ports seems to
ve been their custom of
ing in the autumn to
h for herrings off the
st coast near the mouth
the River Yare, where
e town of Yarmouth
ew up as a result of this
nual visit of the ports-
en. By the time of
illiam the Conqueror
find that they were
und to provide between
em sixty ships to serve

*Seal of Hastings : c. 1220. The ship flying
the banners of the Cinque Ports and of England
has just rammed an enemy ship.*

fifteen days. So valuable were their services considered that
the burgesses of these ports were given the honourable title of
arons', and although the title did not make them peers of the
alm, it did raise them above the rank of ordinary freemen ;
ey also had their own law-courts and assessed their own taxes.
at the most remarkable proof of the honour in which they were
ld was their ' privileges at court '. At a coronation the king
alked from the palace of Westminster to the Abbey and back
Westminster Hall under a canopy, which was supported by
rons of the Cinque Ports, who afterwards sat at the table of
nour on the king's right hand at the coronation banquet and

were allowed to keep the silver staves and silk of the can
which they had carried. These privileges, it may be remark
were exercised down to the time of George IV, and should
procession and banquet be revived at any future coronation
representatives of the Cinque Ports would have the undoub
right to claim their ancient honours, although, with the excep
of Dover, probably none of the ports could produce any ve
more formidable than a fishing-smack.

The ship of Norman times was built high at the bows
stern, and had a central mast with one great square sail. It
steered by a great oar fastened on the right side—the starbo
(=steer-board). Such a ship was converted into a man-of-
by erecting wooden towers at each end—the fore-castle
stern-castle, and fastening a fighting-top (in its simplest f
a large barrel) on the top of the mast. The average crew of
ships collected for the Irish expedition of 1171 was twelve men
a master, but the Cinque Port ships had to carry twenty-
The sailors were a hardy race, accustomed to fighting am
themselves and given to piracy—Chaucer thought no worse
his shipman for his treatment of the crews of the ships he rob
that he would 'send them home by water', in other wo
throw them overboard—and were very indisciplined, often leav
the fleet without permission. Prolonged naval operations w
therefore, never attempted; fleets were got together chiefly
transport troops and occasionally to deal with an enen
squadron that was known to be in the neighbourhood or to
a particular piece of coast.

Other nations used 'galleys', propelled by oars, for fight
but the English do not seem to have favoured this type of ves
though some were built by the three Edwards and by cer
towns, for coast defence; the labour of rowing these galleys
great, and was often performed by criminals and slaves,
possibly this form of slavery did not appeal to the English sp
Our men were skilful at handling their ships, but on sea as
land our successes were due chiefly to the archers, as for insta
in the famous victory over the French at Sluys in 1340.

battle of Sluys was followed in 1350 by the defeat of the Spania
off Winchelsea in a fight which so far resembled the defeat of t
Armada in that the Spanish ships towered over the low-bu
English ; but, contrary to the tactics employed in the Elizabeth
victory, the English on that occasion deliberately came to cl
quarters, grappling their enemies and carrying them by sh
force of arms.

By the end of the fourteenth century ships had much increas
in size and in seaworthiness ; the rudder had replaced the steerii
oar, and the bowsprit had been introduced, causing certa
changes in the rigging. During the next century ships with tw
masts were built, and as the harbours of the Cinque Ports h
silted up and become too shallow for these larger vessels, the Po
ceased to play much part in the formation of fleets. With t
development of Spanish sea-power at the end of this centui
Henry VII saw that if England was to hold her own she mu
have a regular navy and depend no longer upon casual collectio
of armed merchant-ships. Under him, therefore, great men-of-w
were built and the foundations of our navy laid ; and the poli
that he began was carried on on a still larger scale by Henry VI
and Elizabeth, whose ships of English oak, armed with guns
English iron, gave England that supremacy of the sea which s
had first asserted in the reign of John and had claimed with mo
reason under Edward III, but had temporarily lost under l
successors.

X

LAW AND ORDER

FROM time to time our newspapers publish alarming articles on ' a wave of crime ' or ' the prevalence of crimes of violence ', which they attribute to the influence of other papers, cheap novels, ' the pictures ', the War, socialism, the use of drugs, or anything else that they dislike. The occurrence of two or three murders among a population of over forty millions in the course of a month is sufficient to cause such an outcry. If the conditions of the Middle Ages were reproduced for a week or two in modern times the newspapers would have reason for their alarm. When considering the recruiting of the medieval army we saw that in less than a year at the end of the thirteenth century Edward I pardoned 450 murderers—at a time when the population of the country was about five millions. Taking into consideration the number of murderers who were not pardoned—including the large percentage who had avoided arrest—it is obvious that our ancestors held life cheap. Nowadays, also, the use of a knife in a quarrel is apt to be denounced as ' un-English ' ; no doubt it is, but it certainly was not in bygone times, when every one carried a sheath-knife (which he used for his meat) and drew it upon the slightest provocation. An Italian who wrote an account of England in 1496 said, ' There is no country in the world where there are so many thieves and robbers as in England ; insomuch that few venture to go alone in the country, excepting in the middle of the day, and fewer still in the towns at night, and least of all in London.' About the same time also Fortescue found cause for patriotic boasting in the boldness of English criminals :

' It hath ben offten tymes sene in Englande that iij or iiij theves for poverte have sett upon vj or vij trewe men, and robbed them all. But it hath not ben sene in Fraunce that vj or vij theves have be hardy to robbe iij or iiij trewe men. Wherfore it is right selde that Frenchmen be hanged for robbery, for they have no

hartes to do so terable an acte. Ther be therfore more me
hanged in Englande in a yere for robbery and manslaughter tha
be hanged in Fraunce for such maner of crime in vij yeres. The
is no man hanged in Scotlande in vij yere together for robbery
and yet they be often tymes hanged for larceny and stelynge c
goods in the absence of the owner therof. But ther hartes serv
them not to take a manys goods while he is present and wi
defende it—which maner of takynge is called robbery. But th
Englysh man is of another corage. For if he be poor and se
another man havynge rychesse, which may be taken from hyn
by myght, he will not spare to do so.'

It was an age of violence, in which the great men set a ba
example to their inferiors. Leaving out of account the anarch
of Stephen's reign, when every man's hand was against hi
neighbours, and the civil war of York and Lancaster, when th
nobility were divided into rival camps, we find constant feud
between neighbours. At the end of the reign of Henry III th
Earl of Surrey ravaged the lands and assaulted the tenants o
Sir Robert Aguillon ; even under Edward I the Earls of Herefor
and Gloucester were practically at war with one another, fo
which that stern king made them pay dearly ; it is, therefore
not surprising that under his feeble successor there were man
cases of private wars in Lancashire and elsewhere. A century
later we may read in the Paston Letters, which give such a vivi
picture of English life in the fifteenth century, how Norfoll
squires would arm their retainers and attack each other's castles
Even the clergy would seize a disputed church and hold it like
a fortress against the attacks of their rivals. At Oxford and
Cambridge the students of the north and south would fight
pitched battles between themselves, or unite to fight the towns
men. The representatives of the law were defied—but not
always, it must be admitted, with impunity. The story of how
the wild young Prince Hal (afterwards Henry V) insulted
Chief Justice Gascoigne and was promptly committed to prison
by him is well known, even if it is not true ; the first Prince of
Wales was certainly banished from court by his father, Edward I,
for insulting a judge, and the same king made William de Bracse

The Court of King's Bench in the time of Henry VI.

*In front of the justices sit the attorneys and clerks with their scrolls of
parchment, pen-cases, and ink. On the left jurors are being sworn by an usher.
On either side of the prisoner and his jailer are counsel for the prosecution and
defence. In front other prisoners await their turn*

do public penance for similar conduct and imposed a great fine upon Earl John de Warenne, whose retainers had mortally wounded Alan la Zouche in Westminster Hall during the hearing of a suit between him and the Earl. Officials less directly under the king's protection than judges suffered more frequently, and the unfortunate sheriff's officers and bailiffs who had to serve writs on hot-tempered gentry must have become quite used to being assaulted and compelled to eat their own writs.

Such being the lawless state of the country in the Middle Ages, it is worth considering how the authorities attempted to prevent and punish disorder. One of the most important features in the administration of the law was the idea of mutual responsibility. A man who had lands and property which could be seized if he defied the law or fled from arrest had, in a sense, given hostage for his good behaviour; but the bulk of the peasantry, the villeins, had only the use of lands which belonged to their lords. It was, therefore, necessary to find some other hold over them. For those who were servants in the household of a man of position it was simple to make their master responsible for their conduct or at least for their arrest if guilty of any offence. The rest were formed into groups which, as they nominally consisted of ten households, were called ' tithings ' under a ' tithing-man ' or ' head-borough '. If any member of a tithing committed a crime it was the duty of the other members to arrest him and produce him in court when required; if they failed to do so they were fined. Every villein above the age of twelve, who was not a household servant, had to be enrolled in a tithing, kneeling and swearing upon the Gospels, as follows :

' Hear this, Sir steward, that I will not be a thief nor the fellow of a thief, nor will I conceal a theft nor a thief but will reveal it to those to whom it should be revealed; and I will bear faith to the lord King of England, and more especially to my lord, and will be obedient to the orders of his bailiffs.'

Then, having kissed the book, he paid a penny and was bidden to be obedient to the head of his tithing. Special courts were held twice a year to see that this rule was carried out.

Such a court was called a 'View of Frank-pledge[1]' and was originally part of the duties of the Hundred Court, but in course of time it often became attached to the Manorial Court Leet. The View of Frank-pledge inquired into not only the constitution of tithings but also into crimes of violence (murder and bloodshed), suspicious characters (such as persons who were well clothed but had no trade or other known source of income), breaches of the regulations for baking and brewing, the use of false weights and measures, excessive charges (' profiteering ',

Drawing a Traitor to Execution: c. 1440.

as we should call it), and various offences against the customs of the manor. Most of the lesser offences the court could deal with, but the crimes, as a rule, had to be sent up to the assizes, or courts held by the king's justices, who travelled round the country hearing such cases.

A crime, or felony, was a serious offence for which the offender was liable to forfeit his lands and goods and to lose his life or a limb. At the head of all crimes was Treason. ' High Treason ' was at first the attempt to kill or dethrone the king ; later it was extended to cover any plot against the king, even if the plot was not carried out, and under Henry VIII it was even made to

[1] A tithing was also called in Saxon *frith-borh*, meaning ' peace-pledge ' ; the Normans took *frith* to mean ' free ' and translated it into ' frank-pledge'.

include the writing or speaking of words which implied a wish for the king's death or deposition. The punishment for this crime was to be drawn, hanged, and quartered; the criminal was bound hand and foot and drawn through the streets at a horse's tail, usually on a hurdle so that he should not die before reaching the scaffold; he was then hanged until nearly dead; his heart was then cut out and burnt, and his body 'quartered', or cut up, the head being placed in some conspicuous place (the gate-house of London Bridge was usually ornamented with traitors' heads), and in the case of notorious traitors the other portions of the body were often sent to different towns to be exhibited as a warning to others. If the traitor was a woman she was burnt, without drawing or quartering.

'Petty Treason' was the murder of a master by his servant or of a husband by his wife; the punishment was similar to that for High Treason, with the omission of quartering. Blasphemy, heresy, and witchcraft were, in a way, treason against God and were, therefore, punishable with death, but they were offences so rare in England before the fifteenth century that the actual practice of the courts is uncertain; with the growth of the Lollard heresy the continental custom of burning heretics was definitely established by law in this country.

Homicide (man-killing) came eventually to be divided into murder and manslaughter; murder being intentional killing, either unpremeditated or deliberate 'of malice aforethought', and manslaughter being accidental, either culpable, by careless-ness or with intent to do bodily harm but not to kill, or unavoid-able, by the act but against the will of the killer, or justifiable, in self-defence. Primitive law thought only of the result and not of the intention, and in theory regarded all killers alike, but had in practice to lessen or remit the penalty where the act was obviously unintentional; but even the man who killed another in self-defence had to obtain the king's pardon before he could go free. In Saxon times all killing could be atoned for by pay-ment of a fine. This was, no doubt, due to the fact that among a people whose main occupation was fighting homicide was common, and the execution of the offenders would have lessened the fighting strength of the tribe to a dangerous extent. Every man had his definite value, his *wer*; that of the ordinary freeman was 200*s.*, that of the thane 1,200*s.*, those of king's thanes, earls, and others of high rank proportionately higher; this *wer* the slayer must pay to his victim's relations—if he did not they were at liberty to carry on a blood-feud against him and kill him. Moreover, the slayer must also pay a fine to the king for a murder, but apparently not for manslaughter. Under the Normans murder was punished with death, but if the victim was a Norman the whole community, the Hundred, had to pay a heavy fine to the king; and the dead man was assumed to be Norman unless the Hundred could prove his ' Englishry ' to the satisfaction of the coroner, the local representative of the Crown, whose chief duty was to hold inquests on persons found dead. The principle of joint responsibility comes in again in the rule that such inquests should be made by the representatives of the four vills, or townships, nearest to the place where the body was found. They had to report the cause of death and who, if any, were suspected of having caused it, particularly whether the first person to find the body was under suspicion. It is rather amusing to find a jury reporting that a certain man's death was due to his being struck by lightning and going on solemnly to state that his wife, who had found his body, is not suspected of having done it !

In many cases of ' death by misadventure ' the actual cause was an animal or inanimate object—as, for instance, when a child was pushed into the water by a pig, or a man stumbled over a scythe and received a fatal wound. On the Continent it was not unusual to try the offending animal and sentence it to death, but this was not often done in England. Still it was felt that a certain blood-guiltiness attached to the cause of a death, and it was, therefore, forfeited as ' deodand ' (= to be given to God) and its value bestowed in charity for the good of the soul of the deceased ; when the dead man was poor the deodand was often given to his widow or family. In fairness to the non-human agent it was only treated as responsible if there was something corresponding to an act on its part—thus, if a man was so drunk that he fell off a horse that was standing still or out of a stationary boat his death was on his own head, but if horse or boat were moving they were held to have caused his death and were deodand ; therefore, if a man fell under a cart and was killed, not only the cart but also the horses that moved it would be forfeited—but whether the goods in the cart should share the same fate was a question for the lawyers to quarrel over.

Besides murder the other felonies were arson, or house-burning, burglary, or house-breaking, and larceny—the stealing of goods above the value of 1s. For larceny the punishment varied ; the thief caught in the act was almost always put to death at once. Other thieves might escape in Saxon days by paying two or three times the value of the goods stolen ; under the Normans they would lose a foot or a hand, or both ; and from the thirteenth century onward the penalty was death.

Methods of trial were very different in the Middle Ages from what we are accustomed to. One way in which an accused person could clear himself was by ' purgation ' ; for this he had to produce in court a number of men of good standing—six, twelve, or twenty-four, according to the seriousness of the accusation— who would swear that they believed him innocent. This may be called an appeal to the judgement of men, but there was also an appeal to the judgement of God—the ordeal. Such ordeals are common among the less civilized races and may, for instance, be found in the ancient Hebrew laws of the Old Testament. In England there were four main types of ordeals, those by hot iron, hot water, cold water, and by battle. In the ordeal by hot iron the accused had to carry for a distance of three paces a piece of iron of one pound weight, which was heated in the fire while certain prayers were recited ; his hand was then bound up and three days later it was examined ; if it was uninjured he was held to be innocent, but if it was scarred he was guilty and suffered the penalty of his offence. The ordeal by hot water (not apparently much used) was similar, except that the accused had to pick a stone out of a cauldron of boiling water. In the ordeal by water the accused was stripped of his clothes, bound and cast into a pool, over which a priest had recited a prayer that if he were innocent the water would receive him, but if guilty it would reject him ; if he sank he was dragged ashore and released, but if he floated his guilt was considered proved. This particular form of ordeal survived as a test for witchcraft into the seventeenth century and even, unofficially, into the nineteenth. There was another form—the ' corsnaed '—practically never employed,

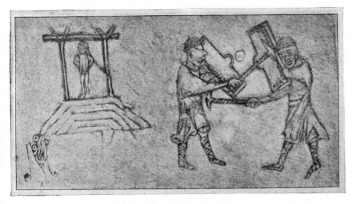

Ordeal by Combat : 1270.

in which the accused took a mouthful of blessed bread, which it was believed would choke him if he were guilty. The best known instance of this is the famous story of how Earl Godwin, being accused of treason, exclaimed, ' If I am guilty may this morsel of bread be my last ! ' and promptly choked and died. The story suffers under the disadvantage of being untrue.

These ordeals continued in use till the reign of John, but by the middle of the twelfth century people were beginning to doubt whether the results were always in accordance with justice. Henry II ordered that a man of notoriously bad character should be banished even if he had passed the test of the ordeal, and when in 1215 the Pope forbade the use of these ordeals he was promptly

obeyed, and they disappeared from our courts of law. One o
their disadvantages had been that they were one-sided, th
accuser running no risk ; the trial by battle was free from thi
objection and continued in use for another century. In an appea
of felony the appellant, or accuser, and the defendant took th
field bare-headed and bare-legged, wearing no armour and eacl
armed only with a staff furnished with an iron horn (like a smal
pick) and carrying a square shield. Before the fight each hac
to swear that he had neither drunk nor concealed about hi
person any charm to defeat the ends of justice. If the accusec
were victorious or could defend himself until nightfall he wa
acquitted and the appellant committed to prison, but if he wer
disabled or compelled to cry ' craven ' in token of defeat he wa
hanged. Ordeal by battle was also used in disputes about th
ownership of land ; in such cases the actual parties to the sui
did not fight in their own person, but by their representatives
or ' champions '. Such champions were bound in theory to b
the free tenants of the disputing parties, but in practice they wer
usually hired men, professional champions, and very well paid
For instance, in 1294 the Dean and Chapter of Southwell, having a
law-suit with Ralph de Frechevile over the advowson of a church
which was to be settled by a duel, hired Roger de Meauton, cham
pion. He was to have 40s. when the case came on and a retainin;
fee of 1s. a day until the date of the duel ; on which day he was to
receive £16 down ; if he only struck ' the king's blow '—a singl
formal blow, enough to carry out the order of the court for a duel
after which the case could be settled by agreement—he shoul
have no more, but if it came to a real fight he should hav
another £16. Other amounts, including the hire of a master, o
trainer, brought his charges up to the large sum of £48—sa
£750 of modern money. Ordeal by battle gradually went ou
of use after the introduction of the alternative of trial by jur
in the reign of Henry II, but by an oversight it was not legall
abolished in cases of felony until 1819, in which year an accusec
felon successfully insisted on his right to defend his case by battle
   The medieval jury was very different from the modern. A

he present time a jury is a body of men who are expected to have
o personal knowledge of the case before them ; they listen to
he evidence and cross-examination of witnesses, the speeches
f the opposing counsel and the summing-up of the judge, and
hen give their verdict, which must be unanimous. In the Middle
Ages the jury were chosen because of their knowledge of the
ase—though objection might be taken to any who were noto-
iously the friends or enemies of either party—they represented
ublic opinion ; when a party to a law-suit appealed to a jury
e was said to ' put himself on the country ', that is to say on the
pinion of the neighbourhood as represented by these twelve men
f good standing. There were no elaborate speeches by counsel ;
he plaintiff, or his attorney, stated his case at full length ; the
efendant replied with a direct denial and then, as a rule, the
ury gave their decision from their own knowledge of the case.
ometimes the defendant would put forward his own version
f the matter in dispute, and sometimes witnesses were called,
ut they simply gave their evidence without cross-examination.

In the matter of felonies there was another type of jury—the
resenting jury—which corresponded more or less to our ' grand
ury ', whose duty it is at the beginning of the Assizes to decide
vhether there is sufficient evidence against the prisoners to
ustify their being put on trial. The presenting jury, who were
he representatives of the vills and hundreds, drew up a list of
ersons who were suspected of any crime. This list was presented
o the justices of the Assizes, who ordered the arrest of all those
amed. The prisoners were then tried by a jury from their own
istrict ; this might very well be composed of the same men as
he presenting jury, but it did not follow that they would be
onvicted ; although the jury had to present any person under
uspicion (on penalty of a fine if they suppressed such informa-
ion), it did not necessarily mean that they themselves believed
he prisoner to be guilty.

The penalty for felony, as we have seen, was death, which was
nflicted by hanging, except in certain towns which had special
ustoms ; in the Cinque Ports and a number of other boroughs

the criminal was drowned ; in one or two places he was throw
off a cliff into the sea ; and in the Scillies he was placed at lo
tide on a rock that was covered by the sea at high tide. Occasio
ally instead of the extreme penalty the felon was deprived
a limb or of his eyes or mutilated in other ways. Lesser mutil
tions were also inflicted for ' petty larceny ' or theft of goo
worth less than a shilling—the commonest being the loss of a
ear ; sometimes the offender's ear was nailed to the pillory an
he had to cut himself free, while among the lead-miners of th
Mendips a thief had his hand spiked to the framework of th
pit-head windlass and had to free himself as best he coul
Mutilation served not only as a punishment but as a warning
others that they were dealing with a bad character, consequent
men who had lost a limb in battle or by accident usually procur
a certificate to that effect ; for instance, we find Edward
certifying that part of the left ear of John de Roghton was to
off by the foot of a horse, and that Robert de Gunthorp lost h
right ear by the bite of a pig when he was lying in his cradle.

Imprisonment was a common form of punishment, and i
light one, for, even taking into consideration the comparative
low standard of comfort in ordinary life, the medieval pris
was often a desperately unpleasant place. In 1315 we fi
a merchant of Lynn complaining of wrongful imprisonment
the jail of Wisbech, ' where by toads and other venomo
vermin he was so inhumanly gnawn that his life was despair
of ', and though we may feel sceptical about the ferocity of t
toads, we know from other evidence that the prisons were oft
full of such, and worse, vermin, dark, damp, and airless. Prison
who had any money or friends could purchase some relief fro
the jailer and could, at any rate, rely on obtaining food, b
the moneyless depended entirely upon the alms of charital
persons. In the larger jails one or two prisoners were allow
to go out and beg food and money for their fellows, and fortunat
the relief of those in prison was one of the ' Seven Acts of Merc
which the Church urged upon the faithful ; but those w
could not or would not fee the keeper of the jail suffered severe

Hanging: c. 1460

The picture represents a legend of how the Blessed Virgin saved the life of a condemned man

Torture, as a punishment or as a means of extracting a confess
of guilt, never formed part of the system of medieval Engl
law. The nearest approach to it was the *peine forte et d.*
applied to those who refused to plead. According to medie
law a trial by jury could only be held with the consent of t
accused; he must 'put himself on the country' (we even fi
a deaf and dumb man pardoned for a murder because it v
impossible for him to do so); if he refused he could not
convicted, but the justices could keep him in prison and ma
life unbearable for him. When certain Dutch sailors w
murdered in Norfolk in 1293 the justices hanged thirteen n
concerned in the crime, but one refused to plead; the senter
upon him, which was that usual in such cases, was that 'on t
day on which he eats he shall not drink and the bread that
has shall be of the worst and the drink that he has (on altern:
days, when he has no bread) shall be filthy water, and he sh
sit upon the bare ground clad only in a linen garment and
shall be loaded with irons from his hands to his elbows and fr
his feet to his knees, until he is willing to submit to trial'. J
about the same time Sir Simon Constable, a wealthy member
a great Yorkshire family, died in prison under this same *pe*
forte et dure rather than submit to trial for having murdered
wife; thereby he died unconvicted and his lands descended
his heirs instead of being forfeited to the king for his felony.

Certain forms of punishment for less serious offences combin
discomfort with exposure to public ridicule or contempt—as,
instance, the stocks and the pillory. In the stocks the offen
sat upon the ground with his feet out in front of him, secured
a wooden frame; in the pillory he stood with his neck faster
in a similar frame, sometimes his hands were also secured in t
same frame; if his offence had made him unpopular he v
liable to become the defenceless mark for stones and garba
The pillory was much used in towns for persons guilty of trad
offences and fraud; bakers, in particular, whose loaves w
under weight were condemned for the third offence to stand in t
pillory. Women, especially ale-wives, guilty of similar offen

re ducked in a pond—the dirtier the better—by means of the
ucking-stool ', a chair fastened to the end of a plank or pole,
d this was also done to those women who misused their tongues
scolding, gossiping or talking scandal—a type of offence
ich seems to have been common in the Middle Ages, strange
it may appear to our modern ideas.

One axiom of legal procedure held good in the Middle Ages as
still does ; that is—first catch your criminal, then punish him.
thing approaching a regular police force existed, and the arrest
criminals depended on the principle of mutual responsibility
eady referred to. The tithing, vill or hundred was responsible

Stocks : c. 1340.

r producing guilty members in court ; moreover, if a murder
s committed in the daytime the vill in which the crime occurred
uld be fined if the criminal escaped. During the night each
l had to provide four men to keep watch and arrest suspicious
aracters—to be out after dark was in itself a suspicious act.
hen a criminal avoided arrest and fled, the ' hue and cry ' was
sed by blowing horns and shouting, and the men of the district,
der the leadership of the constable, who was responsible for
e provision of bows and other arms, pursued the offender to
e borders of their hundred, where they handed on the hue and
y to the constable of the next hundred ; in this way the
iminal might be chased for some distance by relays of pursuers.
the pursuit grew too hot he would frequently take refuge in the
arest church. Once within its precincts he was safe from arrest ;
s pursuers would have to set a watch on the church in case he
ied to escape ; if he remained there for forty days the watch

would become a blockade, no food would be allowed to be broug
to him, and he would be starved into surrender. Usually, he
ever, he sent for the coroner and before him ' abjured the realm
that is to say, he swore to leave England and not return ;
coroner then assigned him a port and he set out at once, carry
a wooden cross in his hand ; he had to go by the direct main ro
to the port and take the first ship leaving the port—if none w
sailing for some time he was supposed every day to walk into
sea up to his knees, as a sign of his endeavour to leave the count
If he turned aside out of the direct road he became at once
outlaw, ' wearing the wolf's head ', and might be slain, like a w
or other vermin, by any one who met him.

While every church possessed this right of sanctuary, there w
certain privileged churches—such as Westminster, St. Martin
le-Grand, and Beverley Minster—whose sanctuary rights e
tended for some distance round the church, and in such pla
there grew up regular settlements of ' sanctuary men ', refug
criminals, who lived there and carried on their several trades
safety so long as they did not venture outside the bounds.
the end of the fifteenth century complaints were made of
abuse of these sanctuaries :

' Unthrifts riot and run in debt upon the boldness of the
places ; yea, and rich men run thither with poor men's goo
there they build, there they spend, and bid their creditors
whistle them. Men's wives run thither with their husban
plate and say they dare not abide with their husbands for beati
Thieves bring thither their stolen goods and live thereon. Th
devise there new robberies ; nightly they steal out, they r
they reave and kill and come in again, as though these pla
gave them not only a safeguard for the harm they have done b
a license also to do more.'

The Church, as a body, extended its protection over all
ordained members. During the twelfth century there w
a great struggle between the Church and the Crown, whi
culminated in the quarrel of Henry II and Becket. The Chur
possessed its own courts, which dealt with all religious and mo
cases ; nor did any one dispute their claim to do so. Beck

owever, claimed that the Church had the sole right to try any
f its members, that is to say any persons who had received
lerical orders, for any offence. As the ecclesiastical courts
ould not inflict any punishment more severe than imprisonment,
his meant that clerical criminals, who were numerous, escaped
ery lightly in comparison with laymen. Henry did not claim
he right of punishing clergy, but urged that a cleric accused of
a crime should be tried by the ecclesiastical court and if guilty
hould be deprived of his orders and handed over to the royal
ourt to be punished as a layman. This Becket absolutely

An escaped criminal taking sanctuary: c. 1340.

efused on the ground that it would be punishing the offender
twice for one offence. The murder of Becket, rousing popular
feeling in his favour, compelled Henry to give way. Eventually
the procedure adopted was that clergy were accused like lay
criminals, but the representative of the bishop was always present
in the court and at once claimed the prisoner as a clerk; the
case was then tried; if the jury acquitted the accused clerk there
was, of course, no more to be said, but if they found him guilty
he was handed over to be dealt with by the bishop. Actually
the guilty clerk would stand a very good chance of getting off,
as the procedure in the ecclesiastical courts was very lax and
inefficient, and the bishops as a rule were not anxious to be
burdened with the cost of prisoners. Originally in order to claim

this ' benefit of clergy ' the accused had to produce his letters of ordination or other definite proof of his being a clerk ; it was only towards the end of the Middle Ages that benefit of clergy was extended to all persons who could read a verse of the Bible correctly, and at all times there were a few offences, notably high treason, for which the accused would be tried by the royal court ' without benefit of clergy '.

XI

INDUSTRY, TRADE, AND FINANCE

THE medieval community was, for its industrial wants, very largely self-supporting. Nowadays the Sussex villager buys earthenware made in Staffordshire, woollen cloth from Yorkshire,

Shops, 15th century.

Draper's, furrier's, barber's, and grocer's shops. Beside the grocer is a sugar-loaf, and over his head an advertisement of 'Good Hippocras' (spiced wine).

cotton goods from Lancashire, boots made in Northampton or Norwich from leather tanned at Bermondsey, tools from Sheffield, and meat from New Zealand. In the Middle Ages his own Downs provided him with mutton and with wool, which his wife spun into yarn, as she spun the hemp and flax from his fields, and wove into cloth ; he or his neighbour tanned the hides of his own beasts with the bark of oaks which he had helped to cut down to feed the furnaces that produced iron for the village blacksmith to make into tools ; and if there was not a potter in his own village he would not have to walk far to buy his crocks of Sussex clay. The modern centralization of manufacture is almost entirely due to the discovery of steam-power. The use of steam to drive machinery made it possible to produce quantities of an article vastly in excess of the requirements of the district in which they were made, and at a price which enabled the maker to bear the cost of sending them great distances and yet sell them more cheaply than hand-made goods could be sold in their place of origin ; and steam also provided the means of distributing the goods from the centres of manufacture to the remotest parts of the country.

It must not, however, be supposed that there was no localization of industry in the Middle Ages. The manufacture of coarse woollen and linen cloth was universal, the tanning of leather practically so, the village smith had a skill, which his modern successor does not have a chance to display, in producing such articles of iron as were commonly required, but pottery could not be made where there was no clay, nor could iron be conjured out of ground that contained no ore. Minerals, in fact, present the most obvious case of necessary localization and, as a consequence, the mining industry shows some very interesting and peculiar features of organization.

The important minerals found in England were iron, lead (usually containing silver), tin, and, from the middle of the thirteenth century onwards, coal. Of these tin was found only in Cornwall and Devon ; lead in Derbyshire, Somerset, and Cumberland ; iron principally north of the Trent and in Gloucester, Sussex, and Kent. Coal, the least valuable in medieval times, was more widely distributed, being worked in most of the northern and western counties from Somerset to Northumberland ; it was also the mineral which required least skill in mining, as it had simply to be dug, while the others, being found in the form of ores, had to be specially treated to obtain the metal. We may, therefore, omit coal-mining and confine our attention to the other minerals. The chief of the peculiar features referred to in connexion with mining was the existence of communities of miners who possessed privileges not shared by other members of the labouring classes. These privileges were due to the value of the products, the skilled nature of the work, and the necessary

Mining: 1561.

Prospecting with the ' divining rods '.

localization of the industry. If a body of workmen make excessive demands upon an employer he can, as a rule, either replace them, if the work is unskilled, or move to some district where the workers are more subservient. But a mine cannot be removed and cannot be successfully worked with unskilled labour. Miners, therefore, have an exceptional pull over their employers, and the rise of privileged mining communities was a feature of the Middle Ages, particularly in Germany, where they became in some cases almost independent states. In England the nearest approach to this is to be found in the tin-miners, owing to the distribution of that metal being so very limited and its value so great. The iron-miners as a whole were not organized ; iron ore was fairly widely distributed, and the digging and smelting of it was not highly skilled labour ; but in the Gloucestershire iron-field of the royal Forest of Dean there was a body of ' free miners ' who had entire control of the mining. They had the right of digging anywhere within the Forest, except in private gardens and orchards or churchyards, provided they paid certain fees to the king and supplied his forges with ore at a fixed price ; and they had their own court, which was held every three weeks, for the settlement of mining disputes. The lead-miners were more highly organized ; each of the three main fields of Derbyshire, Cumberland, and the Mendips had its system of mine courts and code of laws and punishments. They had the right to prospect and to stake out claims anywhere except in churchyards, gardens, and highways ; to demand a right of way, even through growing corn, to their claims ; and to take timber for their mines and furnaces. In the ' stannaries ', or tin-fields, the organization was carried still farther ; the free miners had their own courts and their parliaments, under a warden, which not only passed laws for the stannaries but had the right to veto any national legislation which infringed their privileges. These miners were exempt from ordinary taxation and military service, though they were liable to be taxed separately and enrolled for service (as sappers) under their own officers, and in fact they formed almost a little independent state.

Although no other industry attained such independence, there was a regular system of organization and self-government in most industries. Mention has already been made of the gilds, or friendly societies, which were so numerous in early times. It was natural that persons having the same interests should tend to join the same society or even to form a special society for members of their own trade (just as now there are special clubs which are patronized by, or exclusively reserved for army men, or authors, or actors). In this way there grew up in the twelfth century trade-gilds, which rapidly increased in numbers and importance until they practically controlled the industrial life of the country. Trade- or craft-gilds did in some ways take the place of the modern trade-unions, but the differences between the two organizations are important. A trade-union is composed entirely of the ' workers ' or wage-earning members of the industry, and considers their interests alone ; a craft-gild was composed of both masters and men, employers and employed, and considered the interests of both classes, though with a leaning, which increased towards the end of the medieval period, towards the masters. A trade-union is concerned to obtain good wages for its members, but is not the least concerned to see that they do good work ; a craft-gild was as much concerned for the honour of the industry as for the prosperity of the workers, and aimed at maintaining a high standard of workmanship. A modern trade-union includes the workers in that particular branch of industry all over England ; the medieval craft-gild was confined to a particular town and the regulations for a special trade might vary considerably in different towns.

The typical craft-gild consisted of masters, apprentices, and journeymen. The masters were independent craftsmen with workshops of their own, but not necessarily employers of labour ; they were masters of a craft, not of workmen ; even when a master hired assistants he usually worked at his trade himself. It was not until the fifteenth century that the capitalist employer —the man who provides materials and wages, and sometimes brains, but not the work of his own hands, for the production of goods—became prominent. Before a man could become a master and set up in business he had to satisfy the officers of his gild that he was competent, and usually he had to show that he had been trained for seven years as an apprentice. The apprentices, therefore, were the young men or boys who were learning their trade under a master. Their position in the gild was, naturally, that of inferiors with few privileges ; but the gild looked after their morals and their interests, saw that, on the one hand, they did not gamble or waste their time, and on the other, that their masters taught them their trade, gave them a fair education and did not treat them harshly or beat them more than was reasonable. If at the end of his seven years' training an apprentice wished to become a master he had to pay a certain fee, which was sometimes large ; if he could not afford this and the subsequent expense of setting up he would become a journeyman—a workman hired by the day (French *journée*). In the fifteenth century the journeymen in some trades became so numerous that they formed separate gilds of their own, which the older gilds usually tried to suppress. This increase in the number of journeymen was partly due to the growing attraction of town life, which caused many who would in earlier days have remained on the land to take to trade, partly to the raising of the fee for setting up as a master, and partly to the impoverishment of many smaller masters who were squeezed out by the rising capitalist class and compelled to become journeymen. The gilds did not at first look with favour on these capitalists, and regulations were often passed forbidding any employer to keep more than a certain small number of apprentices and hired servants. A similar effort to prevent the wealthy from monopolizing hired labour was made by the Statutes of Labourers. These Statutes were passed after the Black Death of 1349 had reduced the number of workmen so greatly that the survivors were able to demand wages very much higher than had been customary ; they ordered that workmen should not receive higher wages than they had had before the plague, and by punishing the payer as well as the receiver of high wages endeavoured to keep the wealthy from buying up all the available labour. The Statutes did not succeed in dragging wages down to their former level, and neither they nor the gild regulations could stem the rise of capitalism.

The industry in which the capitalist class was most conspicuous was the cloth trade. By the end of the fourteenth century quite a number of large employers are to be found in Essex and Somerset, and the beginning of the sixteenth century saw the

Craftsmen: 15th century

A Free-mason and a Carpenter proving their skill before a Gild Warden

rise of great clothiers such as John Winchcombe (' Jack of New-bury ', who was fabled to have led a division, composed of his own workmen, to the field of Flodden), the Springs of Lavenham and Stumpe of Malmesbury.   Under these great clothiers the factory system was introduced, by which the workers were brought together under one roof.   Before this the clothiers had given out their work to be done in the workers' own homes, and, indeed, there were often regulations made that no one should own more than a single loom.   The factory system tended to greater efficiency and increased output ;   its chief drawback was that it lessened the freedom and independence of the workers. Looking back we can see that it was the first step in the down-ward path of the wage-earners from the position of craftsmen to that of ' hands '—mere tools to produce goods—which they reached at the beginning of the nineteenth century.   This future consequence was naturally not foreseen at the time ;   nor would it necessarily have been held to outweigh the advantages of increased trade and wealth.   But the smaller manufacturers could see that it threatened their position ;   the gilds, therefore, in most towns endeavoured to maintain a certain equality and restrain the more enterprising employers by passing restrictive regulations.   These merely had the effect of driving the industry out of the towns in which the gilds held sway into the villages, so that in the sixteenth century we find many towns seriously impoverished by the decay of their trade.   Efforts were made to remedy this by passing laws that various industries should only be carried on in boroughs and market towns.   But the story of the struggle between the old-fashioned gilds and the new type of enterprising capitalist employer belongs to the period after the Middle Ages.

Reference has been made to the fact that the gilds looked after the interests of the public by maintaining a good standard of work.   A customer who was dissatisfied with, let us say, the way in which his tailor had made a coat, could appeal to the court of the tailors' gild, and in some cases if a gildsman had undertaken work which he bungled or failed to complete, the other members

his gild would be responsible for carrying it out. And in
dition to attending to complaints the gilds tried to prevent
em by appointing officials to inspect all work done by their
lowship. The best instance of this, and the only one which
s survived to the present day, is found in the case of the Gold-
iths' Company of London. They were granted the exceptional
ivilege of inspecting all the gold and silver work made in
gland (it was unusual for a gild, or company, to exercise
thority outside its own town), and such work is still stamped
th the ' hall-mark '—the leopard's head, which was the mark
the Goldsmiths' Hall—as a guarantee of purity. Sometimes
single article would come under the inspection of several gilds.
us the blade of a silver-mounted knife in a leather sheath
uld be examined by the searchers of the Cutlers' gild, and the
untings by the Goldsmiths; the leather would have had to
ss the Tanners or Leathersellers before it was used and the
eathmakers after it was made up; if it was attached to a belt
e Girdlers' gild would be brought in, and if the belt had a bronze
ckle the Founders would have something to say about it.
the customer who bought that knife and belt ought to be
etty sure of getting a good article, and to ensure his not being
ceived by appearances there were regulations against plating
onze articles with silver or gold. As a further precaution
ainst deceit, workshops had to be open to the public street, and
e selling of goods after dark, when the feeble flickering light
uld enable the dishonest tradesman to palm off bad work upon
e unwary, was forbidden. Also, in order to fix the responsibility
bad work, most articles had to bear the mark of their maker.

It must be admitted that all these precautions were very
cessary, for the standard of commercial morality was low, and
there was any way of evading the regulations and earning
lishonest penny, there were plenty of craftsmen ready to do so.
audulent weights and measures were constantly being seized
the authorities; cloth was so stretched that when it was
tted it would shrink and become useless, or it was so folded
at defects were not visible; pots were made of such base

metal that they melted as soon as they were put on the fir
and everything that could be adulterated was.   It is qu
a mistake to suppose that the medieval tradesman was an hon
and innocent being whose descendants have been corrupted
the commercialism of our age.   The great thirteenth-centu
preacher, Berthold of Ratisbon, whom I have already quot
several times, says :

' Ye that work in clothing, silks or wool or fur, shoes or glov
or girdles ; men can in no wise dispense with you ; men m
needs have clothing, therefore should ye so serve them as to
your work truly ; not to steal half the cloth, or to use other gu
mixing hair with your wool or stretching it out longer, where
a man thinketh to have gotten good cloth, yet thou hast stretch
it to be longer than it should be, and makest a good cloth i
useless stuff.   Nowadays no man can find a good hat for t
falsehood ; the rain will pour down through the brim into
bosom.   Even such deceit is there in shoes, in furs, in skir
a man sells an old skin for a new ; and how manifold are y
deceits no man knoweth so well as thou and thy master t
devil. . . . Thou, trader, shouldst trust God that He will find th
a livelihood with true winnings, for so much hath He promis
thee with His divine mouth.   Yet now thou swearest so lou
how good thy wares are, and what profit thou givest the bu
thereby ; more than ten or thirty times takest thou the names
all the saints in vain—God and all His saints—for wares sca
worth five shillings !   That which is worth five shillings th
sellest, maybe, sixpence higher than if thou hadst not bee
blasphemer of our Lord.   Ye yourselves know best what lies a
frauds are busy in your trade ! '

In one thing our ancestors were wiser than we ; they regar
the tradesman as existing for the benefit of the public and
the public for the benefit of the tradesman.   He served a use
purpose and was entitled to a reasonable profit, but he had
right to take a mean advantage of his neighbour's needs.   No
days the ideal of a trader is, only too often, to buy as chea
as possible and sell for the highest price he can obtain, and
he can ' corner ' an article (i.e. get practically the whole availa
supply of it into his own hands) and charge an extortion
price for it, the height of his ambition is reached ; the m

ho acts up to these ideals is admired and makes a fortune.
the Middle Ages the trader may have had the same ideals,
ut if he attempted to put them into practice he found himself
xtremely unpopular, and probably received his share of home
uths and other even more painful expressions of dislike when
e stood in the pillory. The medieval mind could not see why
 man should be allowed to buy an article cheap and then,
ithout doing anything at all to it, retail it at a very much
gher price. Strong measures were taken against ' forestallers ',

ho bought up goods before
ey came into the open
arket, and ' regraters ', who
ought goods with the object
 selling them again at a
gher price and were prac-
cally shop-keepers in the
odern sense.

The connexion between
dustry (the making of
oods) and Trade (their dis-
ibution) was closer in me-
eval times than at present.
enerally speaking, the man

A Fish-stall. 13th century.

ho made an article sold it in his own shop. It would not be
ually true to say that the man who sold an article had necessarily
ade it, as there were certain goods, such as drugs, spices, or silks,
hich were imported; but even in that case the merchant who
d imported them would sell them direct to the public. The
wholesale house ', supplying goods only to shops, was unknown;
 also was the ' store ', with its innumerable departments, where
ou can buy anything from a pin to a piano. The medieval
aftsman kept strictly to his own trade—the bootmaker might
t mend an old pair of boots nor the cobbler make a new
ir, and the weaver must not dye the cloths he made nor
e dyer weave cloth to dye. The shop was a room on the
ound-floor, with an unglazed window, closed by a shutter

that let down to form a shelf ; within the room would be a tab
or counter, and shelves and hooks for the goods to stand
hang upon.

In addition to the regular shops there were stalls in the marke
which were particularly used for the sale of goods brought
from the neighbourhood. In the larger towns there would
a number of markets or groups of stalls for the sale of particul
goods—such as the fish-market, the corn-market, the cloth-ha
and the ' duddery ' where clothes (still called ' duds ' in slar
were sold. Some goods, especially such things as fruit and fis
were hawked about the streets by costermongers (sellers
' costards ' or apples) and pedlars. ' Chapmen ' also went abo
the country with pack-horses laden with all kinds of small me
chandise—ribbons, knives, mirrors, purses, kerchiefs or scarv
pins and buckles and trinkets of all sorts. As the chapman
his humble way brought the goods of the town shops to the doc
of the manor and the farm, so the merchant brought the goo
of foreign lands to the towns.

Long before the Romans came to Britain the Phoenicians a
supposed to have traded with the natives of Cornwall for t
but what goods they gave in exchange for the metal we do n
know. At the beginning of the Christian era corn was export
from Britain to the Continent, and probably paid for with imp
ments of bronze and cloth of superior quality. Under the Saxo
foreign trade continued on a small scale, but it was the Norm
Conquest that gave the first great impetus to foreign trad
with the lands on either side of the Channel under the same ru
and with Norman merchants settled in London and the otl
trading cities of England the exchange of goods between Engla
and the Continent naturally became greater. The Crusad
drawing men to the wealthy and luxurious lands of the Medit
ranean and the East, brought new ideas and new possibilit
of trade. Silks of Bagdad and Damascus, the fruit and wir
of the Levant, the spices of Alexandria, came to England in t
galleys of the great merchant republics of Genoa and Veni
and were paid for in English cloth and wool. The rich grazi

nds of our damp and temperate island yielded an almost
exhaustible supply of wealth, and the wool and hides of England
rew to our shores the merchandise of all the known countries
f the world. During the fourteenth century the merchants grew

A Merchant engaged on his Accounts : 16th century.

creasingly wealthy and powerful, and at the end of that century
ichael de la Pole, son of a great merchant of Hull, was created
arl of Suffolk, and so began the English tradition of ennobled
erchants. At this time money was becoming plentiful, and many,
specially the richer clergy, who had money to spare, entrusted
to merchants to be used for trading purposes. The merchants
us employed were, at first, usually Italians—members of the

famous families of financiers, bankers, and traders of Florenc
Lucca, and Genoa.

The part played by foreigners in the history of English finan
was remarkable. Owing to the fact that the Church regard
usury—the taking of interest for money lent—as a grievous si
money-lending became the monopoly of the Jews : as their sou
were already irretrievably lost, from the mere fact of their bei
Jews, the Church made no objection to their committing a s
which was so convenient for Christians, who were apt to be sho
of ready money. The Jews have always possessed a genius f
acquiring and manipulating wealth and, in spite of persecutic
they managed to get into their hands a large part of the floati
capital, the actual coin, of the country. They had been broug
into England by the Conqueror, and they remained for tw
centuries under the direct protection of the Crown as usef
though detested, centres of wealth. Towards the end of t
thirteenth century, however, owing to the rise first of the usure
called 'Caorcins' and then of the great Italian financiers, t
Jews ceased to be indispensable and Edward I found hims
able to serve God, without upsetting Mammon, by expelli
the Jews from England. During the reigns of the three Edwar
the Italians constantly advanced large sums to the English kir
and although the fraudulent bankruptcy of Edward III ruin
the great houses of the Bardi and Peruzzi and brought appalli
disaster upon the city of Florence, they continued to play
important part in English finance until the latter part of t
fifteenth century, when, during the Wars of the Roses, the Germ
merchants of the Hanse took their place.

National finance was very different in the Middle Ages fro
what it is now. There was no elaborate system of governme
departments with their 'estimates' and deficits, controlled
a central Treasury department, no yearly 'budget', based
complicated calculations, and no ingenious schemes of taxatic
The national revenue was recognized as belonging to the kir
and, financially, a medieval king might say with Louis XIV
l'état c'est moi. The same account-book would record the wag

id to the army, the money lost by the king in gambling or
ven by him in charity to a blind beggar, the expenses of an
mbassy to a foreign court, and the cost of a pair of slippers
ven to the nurse of the royal children. The royal revenue was
rived from a number of different sources. First there were the
nts of the Crown lands; then there was an uncertain amount
om fines imposed in the law-courts; from the beginning
 the fourteenth century there were also the Customs, particu-
rly the duties on wool and hides exported and wine imported.
hen, owing to war or other causes, the ordinary revenues were
t sufficient, additional sums were raised by loans from foreign
anciers or by 'subsidies'. A subsidy was a percentage tax,
t unlike income-tax, voted by the representatives of those
ho had to pay it—Parliament in the case of the laity, and Con-
cation in the case of the clergy. It was usually at the rate of
 fifteenth or a tenth, but might be as low as a twentieth (a shilling
 the pound) or as high as an eighth (half a crown in the pound).
 was assessed on lands and goods, the representatives of the
mmissioners visiting every house to see the goods and value
em—excepting the armour, jewels, and robes of the gentry,
nd, for lesser persons, one robe for a man and another for his
ife, one ring, one brooch, and one silver drinking-cup.

The money collected from these various sources was accounted
r at the court of the Exchequer, which derived its name from
he great table covered with a chequered cloth, on which the
ccounts were set out and reckoned by means of counters. Many
f the officials who had collected the money were unlearned men
ho would not understand written accounts; even for those
ore learned the difficulty of working out complicated sums in
oman numerals must have been considerable. At the court of
he treasury, therefore, an elaboration of the 'abacus' or calcu-
ting board was in use; this consisted of a table, covered with
 black cloth on which were drawn seven vertical columns,
epresenting, from right to left, pence, shillings, pounds, scores,
undreds, thousands, and tens of thousands of pounds. These
olumns were divided by horizontal lines, cutting the cloth into

a series of squares like those on a chess-board. Within the
squares the accounts were set out with counters. The chancel
and officials sat on one side of the table and the man who
accounts were being checked on the other. The calculating cle
then set out the amount due from the accountant along one li
and the deductions due for expenses and other payments
lower lines. In this way a long and complicated account cou
be easily followed.

The only coin in circulation in England until the end of t
thirteenth century was the silver penny ; 12 of these were call
a shilling, 160 a mark, and 240 a pound ; but there were no coi
corresponding to those denominations. In the fourteenth centu
silver groats (fourpenny pieces) and half-groats were struck, b
the shilling did not make its appearance until the reign
Henry VII. An attempt to introduce a gold coinage was mad
unsuccessfully, by Henry III, but under Edward III gold ' noble
worth 6s. 8d. (half a mark) were struck with a handsome desi
of a ship, and from this time a gold coinage was maintained.

A Jewish Moneylender : 14th century

XII

WOMEN

THE position of women and the attitude of men towards them in the literature of the Middle Ages present some puzzling features and curious contradictions. Woman is at one moment idealized as a divine being, to gain whose love the world may well be lost, at the next she is figured as a worthless and venomous creature, hardly worthy to have a human soul. But, after all, even in our own days there is a considerable difference between the language applied by sentimental novelists to their heroines and that used in comic papers about elderly women. Taking one thing with another, the actual position of women then was not so different from their position at the present day as might at first be supposed.

One feature of chivalry—the code of behaviour of the ideal knight—was the homage paid to ladies. Every young knight and squire with any pretensions to be a man of fashion made a point of being in love when he was not in battle. Whether he devoted himself to one lady or distributed his favours broadcast was not a matter of much importance ; but he was expected to pay exaggerated compliments and display elaborate courtesy to all ladies. So far as this attitude was a mark of respect from the strong to the physically weak, and of homage from the rough man, soiled by contact with the world, to one whom he recognized as purer and more refined, it was good. But unfortunately it was largely an artificial pose, and in particular it was a matter of ' class ' : the knight acknowledged the duty of courtesy towards ladies of his own class, but often he did not consider it necessary to treat humbler women in the same way. Even towards his ladies a knight could upon occasion be astonishingly rude. Nor was the conduct of the ladies quite in accordance with modern ideas ; they were, if anything, more forward than the men in love-making, and pretty nearly their equals in outspoken abuse. Naturally there were plenty of opportunities for scandal to arise, and the opportunities were not neglected, so that in the households of the more fashionable nobles, where chivalry was most professed, it was hard for any lady to keep her reputation unstained.

The worst slanderers of the female sex were the clergy. They could never get out of their heads the part that Eve had played in the unfortunate incident of the apple in the Garden of Eden, and they therefore assumed that as the first woman had brought Sin into the world by tempting Adam, so all women were temptresses and responsible for most of the sins committed by men, and they did not hesitate to say so. The medieval Church, of which all the official members—the clergy, monks, nuns, and friars—were unmarried, lost no opportunity of praising the beauty of celibacy and disparaging married life.

The common people heard women continually abused from the pulpit; if they heard anything on the other side it was likely to be some poem so full of extravagant praise that it lacked all reality. Not unnaturally they had rather a low view of womankind, and popular literature is full of stories and rhymes against women—their fickleness, deceit, extravagance, and above all, their inability to keep either silence or a secret, such as :

> One thyng forsoth I have espied,
> All women be not tong-tied ;
> For if they be, they be belied.
> If ought be sayd to them, certayn,
> Wene you they will not answer agayn ?
> Yea, for every word twayn !

and :

> They be as close and covert as the horn of Gabriel,
> That will not be heard but from heaven to hell.

But such facetiousness is not extinct even now, and we can get a better idea of the middle-class woman and the standard which was set before her by examining a fifteenth-century poem which tells ' How the Good Wife taught her Daughter '. This begins by setting forth the duty of going to church whenever

The Housewife: c. 1520

possible, even in bad weather, and giving alms cheerfully to the poor and sick. It also insists upon proper behaviour in the church, that prayers should be said and there should be no chattering to neighbours. This was a very necessary command, for the behaviour of medieval congregations was shockingly irreverent : men walked about during the service, talking of business or of their travels, ' And ye women ', exclaims a thirteenth-century preacher, ' ye never let your mouths rest from unprofitable babble. One complains to another of her maid-servant, how greedy she is of sleep and how loth to work ; another tells of her husband ; a third of her children, how this one is a weariness, and that other thriveth not.' A later satirist declares that women will not go to church until they have decked themselves out and adorned themselves, and then they spend all their time looking about to see if anybody else is as gaily dressed. The Knight of La Tour Landry, who in 1370 wrote, for the guidance of his daughters, a famous book full of moral stories, reproached the young ladies of his time for taking so long over dressing and doing their hair that they came down too late to attend service. To illustrate his point, he told a tale of a lady who took a very long time to beautify herself and kept the people and the priest waiting so long one Sunday that they cursed her, and as she was looking in her glass at that moment she saw the Devil and was so frightened that she went out of her mind. At the same time the worthy knight thoroughly approved of ' Sunday clothes ' within moderation, and related how a lady was paralysed because she kept her best clothes for feasts and visits, and refused to wear them to church.

The Good Wife next turns to the subject of marriage. She wastes no sentiment over it, but contents herself with telling her daughter to despise no man who does her the honour of wishing to marry her ; to avoid all secrecy about the matter, but to discuss the offer with her friends ; and to be discreet in her behaviour. Marriages were, indeed, for the most part a matter of arrangement, in which the feelings of the bride were very little considered. In particular a wealthy heiress was regarded as

In the Spring

Love-making

a valuable property to dispose of and a good investment to obtain. It was not unusual for parents to arrange marriages for their children while they were still infants ; even the actual marriage ceremony was sometimes performed when the bride and bridegroom were so young that they had to be carried to the church and could not repeat all the words of the service. Such marriages, it is true, were not binding if the parties did not agree when they came to a proper age, but as that age was twelve in the case of girls and fourteen for boys, they were not likely to have very clear ideas about the subject or to resist the wishes of their parents. As such a marriage of infants was only a preliminary to the real marriage, so ordinary marriages were preceded by the ceremony of betrothal, when the man and woman took each other's hand and, in the presence of witnesses, declared their desire to take one another as man and wife, usually celebrating the occasion by an exchange of gifts. Such a betrothal was nearly as binding as an actual marriage, and indeed if a betrothed woman married another man her original partner could legally claim her from her husband. The actual marriage ceremony was very similar to that now in use in the English Church, except that it was performed at the church-porch, and it was only after the ring had been placed upon the bride's finger that the wedding party entered the church for Mass and additional prayers. The wedding was made an excuse for feasting and jollity, especially dancing, the unfortunate bride being expected to dance with any man who asked her, a tiring and unpleasant duty, as open house was kept, and many objectionable characters came for the sake of the excitement and drink.

Once married, the first duty of a wife was to be meek and obedient to her husband. The Knight of La Tour, to impress this on his daughters, tells several stories, including one of a wife who kept contradicting her husband in the presence of strangers, until at last he knocked her down and broke her nose, which completely spoilt her beauty. It is significant that the Knight does not blame the husband or even think it necessary to excuse

A Marriage at the Church Porch: c. 1460

his action. The ideal wife was the patient Griselda, whose story is told by Chaucer's Clerk of Oxford ; raised from poverty to be the wife of a great Marquess, her obedience is tested by him in a variety of ways—she is compelled to give up her children (to be slain, as she believes), to give up her wealth and position, and even to act as servant to the new wife that the Marquess declares he is going to marry ; all of which she does without a murmur, for which her husband praises her and graciously restores her to her former position. Griselda, to modern eyes, is a worm and no woman ; Chaucer himself, though he tells the story charmingly, protests against such meekness, but medieval men with less sense of humour solemnly held her up as a pattern for their wives to follow. The wives, however, seem not infrequently to have preferred to model themselves on Chaucer's far from patient Wife of Bath. That great woman had five husbands, and had ruled them all with a rod of iron —or rather with a tongue of brass, and frankly delighted in the way in which she had tormented, bullied, and tricked them ; yet she professes most admiration and even affection for the husband who beat her and knocked her down. The right of a husband to beat his wife, within reason, was recognized long after the medieval period ; nor was the law in early days so tender towards nagging and scandal-mongering women as nowadays ; ' scolds ' and gossips who annoyed their neighbours could be brought before the local court and punished, usually by being ducked in a convenient pond—the filthier the better— or gagged with a brank.

Whether she was the patient slave, the loving mate or the nagging master of her husband, the married woman was not likely to be idle. The Good Wife has much to say of the duties of the mistress of the house. To begin with, there was the care of the servants, who must be treated fairly, neither too strictly nor too easily ; they were not to be allowed to idle, and they were the more likely to work well if their mistress set them a good example and worked with them. If she belonged to the middle-class and lived in the country she would look after the ierb garden, help with such work as haymaking, go into market with butter, cheese, eggs, poultry, and so forth, make malt and brew ale, and, presumably, do most of the cooking. Even in the houses of the upper class the ladies had a knowledge of cookery, and occasionally put their knowledge into practice.

The Housewife as Cook : c. 1485.

The Knight of La Tour tells how a certain noble knight, who had been on a long voyage abroad, came back with two gowns of the very latest fashion as presents for his two nieces. He went to see one of them, but she took so long making herself smart that he got tired of waiting and rode off, in disgust, to see the other ; she was making bread when he arrived, but as soon as she heard his voice she ran out, with her hands all covered with flour, and embraced him, apologizing for her appearance : he

was so pleased at her display of affection that he gave her bot
the gowns. Even when they did not go so far as to make th
bread, great ladies would make sweetmeats and conserves fro
fruit, and wines and scented waters from flowers. Also the
were skilled in compounding medicines from herbs, which the
administered to their households and to their poorer neighbou
—the lady of the manor being often the unofficial doctor of th
village. Women of lower degree followed their example, an
there were many poor old ' wise women ' whose simple remedie
based on the experience and tradition of centuries, were mo
effective, and even more scientifically sound, than the fearsom
compounds of the professional physicians. Women are eve
found occasionally in the Middle Ages practising as doctor
though naturally the men did their best to suppress them.

The chief occupation of women, however, was spinning
sewing, and embroidery. So universal was spinning tha
' spinster ' became the general legal description of any woma
who had no particular rank or trade and was independent—
that is to say unmarried, for in the eyes of the Law a marrie
woman had practically no existence apart from her husban
Practically all the yarn or woollen thread used for weaving wa
spun in private houses, and the money earned by the womenfol
by spinning was a valuable addition to the income of the peasant
and farmers. Most of this thread was spun with the dista
and spindle, though wheels, turned by hand, came into use i
the fourteenth century, and the modern type of spinning-whee
worked by the foot, was invented in the sixteenth century. Th
distaff was a rod, at one end of which a mass of wool (afte
being cleaned and ' carded ' or combed) was fastened : a littl
of the wool was drawn out and twisted between the fingers t
form a thread, which was fastened to the spindle ; this serve
both as a weight to keep the thread stretched and a reel to win
it on. The distaff was the inseparable companion of the medieva
dame, as knitting-needles were of her modern descendant
during the years of the Great War ; it could be carried unde
the arm or thrust into the waist-belt, and formed on occasio

useful weapon of offence, particularly for the taming of hus-
ands, as medieval artists delight to show; it became the recog-
ized symbol of Woman, and as a king was buried with a sceptre

Ribbon-weaving : the threads of the warp are separated
with the bat-shaped instrument and the bobbin
passed between them : 15th century.

n his hand, so a distaff of silver or gilt wood was placed in the
coffins of the Queens of France. Whether English queens held the
distaff in death is not known, but that they did in their lifetime
s certain, and Eleanor of Castile, the gracious queen of Edward I,
practised the further art of weaving. Generally speaking, however,

weaving was done by men, and we may assume that the material
woven by royal and gentle ladies were either tapestries, silk
ribbons, or light stuffs possessing beauty rather than strength.

Naturally the care of children was not the least of the married
woman's tasks; but our Good Wife dismisses this subject in
a couple of verses—one to the effect that if children are dis-
obedient you should not curse them or box their ears, but take
' a smert rodde ' and beat them till they cry for mercy; the
other advising the mother, as soon as daughters are born, to start
saving up for their marriage, and to get them married off as
soon as they are old enough.   The anxiety of English parents
to get rid of their children was unfavourably commented upon
by Italian visitors in the sixteenth century, who noted with
surprise that the English would send their children of seven or
eight years old to be brought up in great households (the equivalent, as we have seen, of modern boarding-schools) or to be
apprenticed to some trade.   The education of girls in the Middle
Ages is a subject about which not a great deal is known.   Owing
to the absence of any institutions for girls corresponding to the
grammar-schools for boys, it is probable that few women of the
middle and lower classes had any kind of education.   On the
other hand, in the noble and wealthy classes of society the proportion of girls who could read and write was high.   In medieval
romances and pictures ladies are constantly represented as
reading books, and the private accounts of the royal household
from the days of Edward I downwards contain many entries of
the purchase of ' A B Cs ', writing-tablets, and so forth for the
young princesses and of books for the queens and other ladies.
Many nunneries acted as boarding-schools for young ladies, but
their instruction was probably limited to the reading and writing
of English and of French (' of Stratford-atte-Bowe ' rather than
of Paris, as Chaucer says of his Prioress), few nuns having any
knowledge of Latin, so that science and solid learning was out
of their reach.   While it is interesting to note that the first
medieval dramatist was a nun—Hroswitha of Gandersheim—
and that some of the most charming short romances were written

n the twelfth century by Marie de France, there is hardly
nother woman author of any note, with the exception of
Christine de Pisan (at the end of the fourteenth century), to be
ound in medieval Europe.

Returning to our Good Wife, we find her warning her daughter
not to be jealous if she sees her neighbours better dressed than
herself, and not to spend more than her husband can afford
over dress. As we might expect, the worthy Knight of La Tour
has a good deal to say on the subject of dress ; like most men
he could not see the sense of women putting fur round the
bottom of their skirts, where it dragged in the mud and only
kept their heels warm, instead of round the more delicate parts
of their bodies which required protection from the cold ; but,
unlike many men, he did not pretend to lay down the law about
fashions for any women except his own daughters and his household. To his daughters his sensible advice was that they should
follow the approved fashions worn by persons of good standing
and not try to lead them by aping those flighty women who
were for ever adopting new and immodest costumes. A century
earlier, Berthold of Ratisbon, the most brilliant of medieval
preachers, had denounced the love of dress as the chief snare
for women's souls :

' In order that ye may compass men's praise ye spend all your
labour on your garments—on your veils and your kirtles. Many
of you pay as much to the sempstress as the cost of the cloth
itself ; it must have shields on the shoulders, it must be flounced
and tucked all round the hem ; it is not enough for you to show
your pride in your very buttonholes, but you must also send your
feet to hell by special torments, ye trot this way and that way
with your fine stitchings. Ye busy yourselves with your veils,
ye twitch them hither, ye twitch them thither ; ye gild them
here and there with gold thread ; ye will spend a good six months'
work on a single veil. . . . When thou shouldest be busy in the
house with something needful for the goodman, or for thyself,
or thy children, or thy guests, then art thou busy instead with
thy hair, thou art careful whether thy sleeves sit well, or thy veil
or thy headdress, wherewith thy whole time is filled.'

To attempt to deal with the changing fashions in women's

dress during five hundred years in about the same number of words would be absurd, nor can any amount of description be so satisfactory as a few pictures, so that the illustrations in this book may be left to speak for themselves in this matter. In one thing only were the ladies consistent throughout the whole period, and that was in wearing long skirts; only peasant women who worked in the fields wore skirts above their ankles even quite young children wore long skirts; which is rather remarkable when one considers the filthy state of the roads and even of the floors—but fashions are not, or at any rate were not, affected by considerations of common-sense. This is particularly obvious in the case of the head-dresses of the fifteenth century, the period of the greatest luxury and extravagance in dress. At this time ladies of fashion went in for enormous head dresses, like great horns, projecting upwards and outwards, so that they could with difficulty pass through an ordinary door a little later these twin horns gave way to a towering steeple or extinguisher-shaped head-dress with a veil attached. Preachers denounced them in vain, satiric poets wrote rhymes, bidding women cast their horns away, without effect, but it would seem that when irreverent street urchins took to hooting and jeering at their wearers the fashion fell out of favour. With these steeple head-dresses went another strange freak of fashion, the plucking out of all the front hair, so as to carry the forehead right up on to the top of the head, producing an effect which was much admired at the time but is very unattractive to modern eyes. At other periods it was fashionable to have masses of hair, and those who were not so favoured by nature used false hair, and even wool. And at all times the use of face paints and powders was common.

Such fashionable follies did not greatly affect the respectable middle class to which our Good Wife belonged, but they had their own weaknesses, and it sounds rather strange to us to find her advising her daughter not to get drunk often:

> And if thou be in place where good ale is on lofte,
> Whether that thou serve thereof, or that thou sit soft,

The Steeple Head-dress : c. 1470

Moderately thou take thereof that thou fall in no blame,
For if thou be oft drunk it falleth thee to shame.
　　For they that be oft drunk,
　　Thrift is from them sunk,
　　　My dear child.

There is, however, plenty of evidence that women frequented the taverns as men did : often quite blamelessly, for the medieval tavern was the equivalent of the modern tea-shop. Moreover many of the taverns were kept, and practically all the ale was brewed, by women. These ale-wives were notorious for their trickery, adulterating the ale and selling by false measures.

Another trade that was almost entirely in the hands of women was the silk industry. The rich and splendid silks, satins, velvets, and damasks worn by the wealthy were practically all imported, mostly from the East, but smaller silk goods, such as ribbons and girdles, were woven by the women, who were also skilled at embroidery, and girls of gentle birth occasionally learnt the art as apprentices to these silkwomen. The number of women who were in trade in one way or another in the Middle Ages was considerable, though in many cases they seem to have been the widows or daughters of men who had founded the business, and they probably left most of the actual management to a foreman. All the trade gilds seem to have admitted women as members, and they often kept small retail shops and still more often sold such goods as fish and vegetables or fruit at stalls in the markets. Occasionally they are found helping with the less laborious duties at the mines—such as washing the ore—but it was left to the eighteenth and nineteenth centuries to exploit the cheap labour of women and children in the slavery of mines and factories.

As women shared in the labours of the men, so they also joined in their amusements and sport, particularly in hawking and hunting the deer, shooting with a light bow and catching rabbits with the aid of nets and ferrets. Naturally, also, they played their part in the gentler forms of amusement, dancing, singing, and music, both indoors and even more outside in the fields or gardens. Ladies spent much of their leisure time in their gardens, and medieval artists loved to picture them there, talking, singing, or gathering flowers and weaving them into chaplets for the adornment of their heads. Then, when opportunity offered, they would attend such exciting events as tournaments, encouraging the performers and rewarding the successful knights by giving them prizes, usually jewels. Sometimes they would take part in a gentle form of tournament in which a castle was set up to be defended by ladies, who used flowers as the missiles with which they bombarded the attacking knights. Nor were they incapable of taking part in sterner warfare. Apart from the exceptional case of Joan of Arc, there were plenty of instances of ladies who, if they did not lead their troops into battle, at least defended their castles against attack, such as Nicholaa de la Haye, who gallantly held Lincoln Castle for the royalists in 1217, and Lady Joan Pelham, who kept Pevensey Castle for Henry IV in 1399, or the nameless women who with stones and boiling water kept the Scots from storming the walls of Carlisle.

Husband-taming.

In love and war, in the house and the field, in sport and business, medieval women played their part with the men, sharing in their activities to a degree not so very inferior to that of women at the present day.

XIII

WAYFARING

IN the second half of the nineteenth century and almost down to the beginning of this present century it was quite usual to find that a large proportion of the inhabitants of the smaller villages had never been twenty miles from their native parish. It might naturally be supposed that if this was true in days when roads were good and railways had been built all over the country the proportion of untravelled Englishmen would have been very much greater in medieval times. But this was far from being the case ; men in the Middle Ages travelled and moved about the country more than they did in more recent times. Apart from those whom we may call professional wanderers—the chapmen or pedlars, tramping the country with their wares, the strolling musicians, acrobats and players, beggars, and so forth—the ordinary villagers had many reasons for going outside their parish bounds. Pilgrimages, of which we shall have more to say, drew many even to cross the seas, and as a rule all pious parishioners were expected to go to the cathedral, or some other great church, of their diocese, on one or more special festivals of the year. Then the law compelled a great number of freemen, the reeve and four men from each vill, and various jurors and others to attend the County Court. If war broke out—and there were few years in which there was no war—every able-bodied man in a wide district might be hurried off to repel an invasion, and in any case a considerable number of men would be called up from all over the country to muster at some particular place, and possibly to go across the sea to France or Flanders. The great fairs, also, where alone it was possible to buy so many things that the villages, and even the towns, did not produce, acted as magnets to draw men from near and far, on their own business or on behalf of their manorial lords. In almost every manor there were men who held land in return for which they had to do carrying service with carts or pack-horses, which might involve journeys of considerable length. Great landowners, also, had estates in half a dozen different counties, and between these estates there was a continual movement of labourers, bringing provisions to the manor at which the lord happened to be, or moving cattle from one manor to stock another.

Owing to the lack of any distributing organization the difficulty of feeding a great household, outside such great ports as London, was serious. This was one of the reasons why the royal court when not at Westminster or Winchester is usually found moving rapidly through the country, rarely staying more than two or three days in one place. The early Plantagenets in particular moved about with a rapidity which is astonishing, suggesting rather these days of motor-cars than the leisurely days of lumbering wagons. An unhappy member of the court of King Henry II has left a vivid description of the discomforts of following that restless monarch ; how the king would announce his intention of stopping at some town and then would suddenly change his mind and push on to some small place, where late arrivals would find all the lodgings occupied and all the food commandeered ; when at last they had found a place to rest and something to eat, the order would come to move on, things that had hardly been unpacked would have to be corded up again, and the wretched courtiers would have to mount and ride, leaving their meal still cooking. King John resembled his father in the rapidity of his movements. When, on the other hand, the court did settle down for a longer stay the neighbourhood suffered ; all surplus provisions were soon used up, and the royal ' purveyors '—the officers charged with the duty of obtaining supplies—seized what they wanted and paid what they chose, which was often nothing. In Saxon days arrangements had been made by which a number of royal manors, instead of paying money rents, had to provide food and lodging for the king and his retinue for one or more nights every year. This idea was copied after the Conquest by some of the nobles, and we find estates held by the service of entertaining the lord a certain number of times or on specified occasions.

The retinues of the great lords were large, often enormous. Even such comparatively humble persons as archdeacons, when making their parochial visitations, had a way of travelling with a train of twenty or thirty horsemen, whom they expected the local monasteries to lodge and feed free of charge. Princes and nobles would think nothing of travelling with two or three hundred retainers. When Thomas Becket, at that time Chancellor, was sent on an embassy to France in 1158, he had two hundred knights, clerks, esquires, and noble youths, splendidly attired and mounted, each with his own servants; besides these there were eight great carts drawn by five horses, with a man to each horse, in addition to the driver, twelve pack-horses with their grooms, and men with watch-dogs, greyhounds, and hawks. It is no wonder that the French were impressed with the magnificence of the English king, whose chancellor travelled with such a retinue.

The existence of this continual flow of traffic from one part of the country to another suggests that there must have been an elaborate and efficient system of roads. Such a system the English owed to the Romans, whose habit it was to construct in all parts of their empire a network of splendid roads, by which they could move their troops rapidly from one place to another. The Romans were a thoroughly practical race, and had brought the science of engineering and road-building to a high pitch of excellence. Their roads were most elaborately constructed, the surface in some cases being paved with stone, and were built to last; which they did so effectually that they remained in use all through the Middle Ages, when the art of road-making had been completely lost. In addition to these built roads, carried across the country from town to town with mathematical accuracy and directness, there were in the hilly districts 'ridge-ways' and tracks running along the crests of the hills, usually pre-Roman in origin, but often improved by the Romans. As to the lesser roads, connecting the great highways with one

another and with outlying villages, they were not so much roads
as strips of land left for the passage of traffic. If the ground
was stony and the weather fairly dry they would be passable ;

Old London Bridge.

if the soil was a heavy clay and there was much rain, the traveller
whose horse was not exceptionally powerful ran considerable
risk of being bogged.

The chief obstacles to traffic were rivers and streams. In the
earliest times these could only be crossed at points where they

were shallow, by means of fords; these were inconvenient and dangerous when the waters were swollen by much rain, and under the Romans many fords were replaced by bridges. The importance of bridges was so well recognized by the Saxons that one of the ' three necessary duties ' imposed upon all land-owners was the repair of bridges. In later times the influence of the Church was employed to the same end; religious gilds were formed to build and maintain bridges; bishops granted ' indulgences '—remission of so many days' penance for sins—to those who contributed money or labour for the same purpose; and hermitages or small priories, such as that of ' St. Bartholo-mew of the Causeway ' at Arundel, were founded, of which the brethren had to collect alms from passers-by for the repair of the bridge. To point out the religious duty of thus assisting wayfarers, and also to protect the bridge by placing it under the guardianship of a particular saint, it was a common practice to build a chapel upon the bridge—examples of which still remain at Wakefield and St. Ives and a few other places. For the protection of bridges, or rather of the towns to which they led, against attack, fortified towers were sometimes placed at one or both ends. The most famous of all English bridges, London Bridge, had both chapel and tower, and was also lined on each side with houses, which overhung the river, and occasion-ally fell down into it. This bridge was begun by a priest, Peter of Colechurch, in 1176, to take the place of an earlier wooden bridge which had become ruinous. It was carried on twenty arches (the first of which was discovered, embedded in later masonry, in 1922), and included a drawbridge, which could be raised either for the defence of the city or to allow ships to pass. London Bridge was justly regarded throughout the Middle Ages as a triumph of engineering, and continued to be one of the most striking features of the city until its picturesque houses were destroyed in the terrible Fire of London in 1666. During the period of its existence, however, it more than once suffered considerable injury, the most serious disaster occurring in 1281, when exceptional frost and snow led to the breaking of five

arches. Many other instances of bridges falling or even being
swept completely away are recorded, and in spite of the Law
and the Church they were often allowed to get into such a state
of disrepair that they were a danger instead of a blessing to
unwary travellers.

Dangers of another sort also beset the medieval traveller.
Where his road ran through wooded country he had to be ever
on his guard against attack by wild beasts or wilder men. In
Saxon days Leofstan, who was nicknamed ' Plumstone ', twelfth

Wayfarers : c. 1300.

abbot of St. Albans, is recorded to have cut down thick woods
on either side of Watling Street which sheltered wolves, boars,
wild bulls, and stags, and even worse, thieves, robbers, brigands,
outlaws, and fugitives from justice. Even as late as 1281 wolves
and outlaws are coupled together as vermin, sheltered by certain
woods which the Abbot of Gloucester was licensed to cut down ;
and if wolves ceased soon after that date to be a serious menace,
robbers continued to flourish for another five centuries or so.
A medieval example of that picturesque but unpleasant figure,
the highwayman, is found in 1417, when a chronicler records
the arrest of the parson of Wortham in Norfolk, who had long
haunted Newmarket Heath and there robbed and spoiled many
of the king's subjects. He was but one of a very long list of

such robbers, and by no means the only one in holy orders. The most famous, however, of all the medieval gangs of highwaymen were ' the robbers of Alton ', who infested the wooded valley through which the high road runs to Winchester, and terrorized the countryside in the days of Henry III. For some years they carried on their evil practices with impunity, pillaging merchants, both foreign and English, with much profit to themselves ; but at last they waxed so bold as to seize the king's wine on its way to Winchester. Henry's rage was unbounded ; Justices were appointed to discover and punish the offenders ; the first jury, who refused to denounce anybody, were clapped into prison ; a second jury, warned by the fate of their predecessors, made a full report, incriminating all classes from poor peasant women who had cooked food for the outlaws under compulsion, up to members of the king's own household, and including some of the wealthiest merchants of Winchester. A good number of offenders were caught and hanged, others fled, forfeiting their property, others were fined, the woods on either side of the road were cut down, and the pass of Alton lost its terrors for wayfarers.

With the exception of those who, for reasons of poverty, fared on foot, practically everybody travelled on horseback. Even the most part of merchandise was carried by pack-horses. For a man to ride in a cart was a mark of indignity or ill health. Prisoners and wounded men might be placed in carts—lumbering, springless affairs with massive wheels, of which the rims were studded with large-headed nails. Occasionally an old or sick man might travel in a litter, a sort of covered-in stretcher, to the poles of which horses were harnessed, one in front and one behind ; in such a litter, glittering with paint and gilding and cushioned and curtained with rich silks, Edward I set out on his last journey to Scotland. Delicate ladies also would sometimes journey in state coaches—great four-wheeled wagons with arched coverings of painted canvas, drawn by half a dozen horses. With these exceptions all rode. The ladies, as a rule, rode side-saddle, except when hunting or for any other reason

riding fast, when they would ride astride. Thus when the
Empress Maud was retreating from Winchester, her escort, finding that the enemy were pursuing, insisted that she should put
her leg over the saddle-bow, as it was impossible to go fast
sitting sideways. Women of lower rank also seem usually to
have ridden astride, as in a famous fifteenth-century series of

A Prisoner in a Cart: 1450.

*The victorious army welcomed by a procession of clergy; the walls of the town hung with
silks and tapestries.*

drawings of Chaucer's characters, while the Prioress rides sideways, the Wife of Bath sits astride.

In medieval England, as now in the East and in the colonies,
hospitality was recognized as a virtue and a duty. The benighted
traveller might usually feel assured of a lodging at almost any
house at which he liked to knock, though naturally the warmth

and comfort of his welcome would vary greatly. The monasteries in particular, acted as hotels for the wealthy, and casual wards for the poor, special buildings being set apart for the reception of travellers. In all the towns and along the main roads there were regular inns and hostelries, where a bed of a kind, or, if the house were crowded, a share of a bed could be obtained and also food and, above all, drink. They were not luxurious, but the medieval traveller was not particular, and if his bed was well supplied with clean straw and fairly free from fleas, he counted himself lucky.

It was at the Tabard Inn in Southwark that Chaucer's company of thirty persons assembled to set forth on their pilgrimage to Canterbury. As already mentioned, pilgrimages were one of the main incentives to travel in the Middle Ages. The instinct of hero-worship, which leads us nowadays to visit Stratford-on-Avon to see Shakespeare's house, to go to Portsmouth and gaze upon the spot where Nelson fell on board the *Victory*, or to thrust ourselves forward that we may acquire the autograph of some famous cricketer or actor, was in the Middle Ages concerned entirely with religion. Genuine admiration of the lives of holy men and women led in the first place to the desire to possess, or at least to see, objects that had belonged to them— a comb, a pair of shoes or a girdle, or, better still, a tooth or a bone from their bodies. Then grew up the belief that these objects had in some way inherited the virtues and powers of their saintly owners, and that through them miracles were wrought. This belief, encouraged by the Church, took a firm hold on the popular imagination; such relics were placed in shrines, elaborately carved and glittering with gold and jewels which became the chief ornaments and chief centres of devotion in the churches. Astonishing cures were performed upon the sick and diseased who worshipped at these shrines, perhaps by the merits of the saints or perhaps by the faith of the worshippers and the news of such miracles was published far and wide, not without exaggeration, by the clergy, who took therefrom no small profit in the offerings of pious visitors. When once a shrine

The Shrine of St. Edmund
Visit of Henry VI in 1433

The Shrine of St. William of York : c. 1400. A man whose leg has been healed offers a model leg ; other votive offerings hang by the shrine

had gained a reputation for miracles a steady stream of pilgrims would flow towards it. Not all the pilgrims were seeking bodily health ; more were concerned to obtain the spiritual benefits promised to those who worshipped, and gave money, at the shrines —here so many days relaxation of penance, there so many years release from purgatory ; others were simply intent on sight-seeing, and glad to make devotion an excuse for visiting distant towns or foreign lands. On arriving at their destination the pilgrims would leave their luggage and horses, if such they possessed, at an inn and make their way to the church, where they would wander round, gazing at the monuments and trying to puzzle out the subjects of the stained-glass windows. The keepers of the shrine would show them the shrine itself, pointing out jewels that had been given by kings or great nobles, and would show them, and possibly allow them to kiss, certain relics, telling them of the miraculous cures which had been performed there, in evidence of which they would point to the hanging rows of votive offerings—models of legs and arms, of ships and so forth—given by those who had recovered the use of their limbs or been saved from shipwreck and other dangers by the intervention of the saint. The pilgrims would pay their devotions to the saint and their alms to the keepers of the shrine, and would then buy leaden badges stamped with the symbol of the shrine—a cockle-shell for St. James, a W for Walsingham, an arrow for St. Edmund, or a figure of an archbishop for St. Thomas of Canterbury. These badges they fastened in their hats as signs that they had visited that particular shrine. Many beggars accumulated quantities of such badges, and on the strength of the sanctity which they had acquired by performing so many pilgrimages, extorted undeserved alms from the devout. So in *Piers Plowman* a typical palmer, or pilgrim, is described as

In pilgrim's dress apparelled ; he had a staff in his hand,
Bound with broad list like bindweed twisted round it,
A bowl and bag he bare at his side,
And on his hat a hundred flasks of lead,
Many a cross from Sinai, scallop-shells of Spain,

Fishing-boats of the fifteenth century

Cross-keys from Rome, and the portraiture of Christ,
Signs of his pilgrimage, that men might know his saints.
The folk required of him whence he had come.
' From Sinai ', says he, ' and from our Lord's Sepulchre,
Bethlehem, Babylon, Alexandria, Armenia, and Damascus
Ye may see by my signs that be upon my hat
Good saints have I sought for my soul's health,
Walking full wide in wet and dry.'

In England the greatest of all pilgrimage centres was the shrine of St. Thomas Becket at Canterbury, the wealth of which in its adornments of gold and jewels at the time when it was seized by Henry VIII amounted to about a million pounds of modern money. An Italian visitor in 1496 says :

' The magnificence of the tomb of St. Thomas the Martyr, Archbishop of Canterbury, surpasses all belief. This, notwithstanding its great size, is entirely covered over with plates of pure gold ; but the gold is scarcely visible from the variety of precious stones with which it is studded, such as sapphires, diamonds, rubies, and emeralds ; and on every side that the eye turns, something more beautiful than the other appears. And these beauties of nature are enhanced by human skill, for the gold is carved and engraved in beautiful designs, both large and small, and agates, jaspers, and cornelians set in relief, some of the cameos being of such a size that I dare not mention it. But everything is left far behind by a ruby, not larger than a man's thumb nail, which is set to the right of the altar. The church is rather dark, and particularly so where the shrine is placed, and when we went to see it the sun was nearly gone down and the weather was cloudy ; yet I saw that ruby as well as if I had it in my hand ; they say it was the gift of a king of France.'

The shrine of the Blessed Virgin at Walsingham almost equalled that of St. Thomas in fame and wealth, and others, such as those of St. Alban, St. Edward the Confessor at Westminster, St. Edmund at Bury, and St. Cuthbert at Durham were not far inferior. For the more venturesome there were possibilities of acquiring much merit and some reputation among their less travelled neighbours, at the expense of much discomfort and even danger, by visiting shrines in distant lands. Naturally the

Here shewes howe good prouision made of englissh clothe and
other thynge necessary and licence hadde of the kyng. Erle
Richard sailed towardes the holy lond and   specially to the
holy Cite of Jherlm Where our lord Jhu   Criste wilfully
suffered his bitter passion for the redempcion   of al man
kynde.

The Earl of Warwick starting on a Pilgrimage: c. 1475

*The sail of the ship bears the arms of Beauchamp quartered with Newburgh;
the standard has the ragged staff, the Earl's badge*

first place was given to the Holy Land of Palestine, where there were so many spots sanctified by their connexion with the life of Christ, as well as many not so much holy as interesting, such as the graves of most of the Old Testament worthies, the cave containing the beds of Adam and Eve, and the pillar of salt that had once been Lot's wife. Next in sanctity and interest came Rome with its scores of churches and thousands of relics. Guide-books to the sacred sights of Rome were compiled for the use of pilgrims at least as early as the fourteenth century, and were, no doubt, in great demand. The most popular of all foreign pilgrimages, however, was that to the shrine of St. James of Compostella in Spain. While some went thither by land, journeying slowly through the whole length of France, most went by sea, and the transport of pilgrims from English ports to Spain was a brisk and prosperous business. No little courage must have been needed to face the stormy Bay of Biscay in the little medieval ships, which to a modern sailor would seem hardly more seaworthy than the cockle-shells which formed the badge of the pilgrims of St. James. With their high prows and sterns and their single mast, carrying a great square sail, the vessels of the Middle Ages must have been hard to handle in any but a following wind. Till the end of the fourteenth century the steering was done by a great oar, or paddle, fastened on the right side of the stern, and although the compass, or mariner's needle, was known in the twelfth century, it does not seem to have been in common use until quite the end of the Middle Ages. The accommodation on these ships must have been at best very limited and cramped, and although our ancestors were a hardy race, they were no more free from sea-sickness than their descendants. A humorous poet of the fifteenth century has left a description of the sea voyage to St. James which puts the troubles of the unhappy pilgrims before us very vividly :

> Men may leave all games,
> That sail to St. James !
> For many a man it gramys (=grieves)
>   When they begin to sail.

For when they have taken the sea,
At Sandwich or at Winchelsea,
At Bristol or where that it be,
  Their hearts begin to fail.

Then comes a spirited description of the captain calling his orders and the men shouting as they haul on the ropes.

This mean while the pilgrims lie,
And have their bowls fast them by,
And cry after hot malvesy (=malmsey wine)
  Their health for to restore.

And some would have a salted toast,
For they might eat neither boiled nor roast
A man might soon pay for their cost
  As for one day or twain.

Some laid their books upon their knee,
And read so long they might not see ;
' Alas ! my head will cleave in three ! '
  Thus saith another certain.

A sack of straw were there right good,
For some must lie down on their hood.
I had as lief be in the wood
  Without meat or drink ;

For when that we shall go to bed,
The pump is nigh to our bed's head ;
A man were as good as to be dead
  As smell thereof the stink !

It is not surprising that many pious persons preferred to perform their pilgrimages by proxy, and sent men out to visit the shrines and offer the necessary prayers on their behalf, either in their lifetime or more often after their death. Legacies for such a purpose are of common occurrence in medieval wills. As early as 1274 a London citizen, Geoffrey Godard, left money for a man to be sent to the Holy Land on the occasion of the next general pilgrimage, and in 1352 a London merchant left £20 for pilgrimages to be made to either the Holy Sepulchre or Mount Sinai, and £7 for one to St. James. A century later a Yorkshire rector ensured the safety of his soul by a wide distribution of his favours, providing for pilgrimages to the famous Rood, or Crucifix, at the North Door of St. Paul's, another Rood at Thorpe Bassett, the shrines of the Blessed Virgin at Walsingham, Lincoln, Guisborough, Carlisle, Scarborough, and Doncaster, St. Thomas of Canterbury, St. Etheldreda of Ely, St. William of York, St. John of Beverley, and the other St. John of Bridlington, St. Ninian of Whithorne in Scotland, and a few other saints. Katherine of Aragon, the divorced wife of Henry VIII, left money for a man to visit ' Our Lady of Walsingham ', though the prayers for her soul can hardly have ceased to echo through the church before her husband's ruthless hand fell upon Walsingham and swept the treasures of the shrine into his coffers.

BIBLIOGRAPHY

No attempt will be made here to give anything approaching a complete list of the books which have been written on the subjects upon which I have touched. I am content to indicate a few books which will be found useful by students, or teachers, who wish to learn more about matters which I have, inevitably, treated in merest outline. Many of these books will be found to contain fuller Bibliographies of their own.

As the Middle Ages are best seen through the eyes of contemporary writers I gave first place to two books by G. G. Coulton—*A Medieval Garner*, and *Social Life in Britain from the Conquest to the Reformation*. Both consist of extracts from medieval writers, in the original English or in translation, dealing with every side of life ; the *Social Life* is arranged according to subjects, while the *Garner* has no kind of arrangement, but affords fine mixed feeding.

Of books dealing generally with my subject, H. W. C. Davis's *Mediaeval England* and Traill's *Social England* both contain good articles and excellent illustrations. Miss Power's *Medieval People* and Quennell's *History of Every-day Things* are both very readable and illuminative. Mention may also be made of Cutts, *Scenes and Characters of the Middle Ages* ; Abram, *English Life and Manners in the Later Middle Ages* ; Coulton, *Chaucer and his England* ; Trevelyan, *England in the Age of Wyclif* ; H. S. Bennett, *The Pastons and their England*.

For ' Country Life ' : Harold Peake, *The English Village* ; Seebohm, *The English Village Community* ; Vinogradoff, *Villeinage in England* (for advanced students) ; Orr, *History of Agriculture* ; Thorold Rogers, *Six Centuries of Work and Wages*.

For ' Sport ' : Strutt, *Sports and Pastimes* (ed. Cox) ; Baillie-Grohman, *The Master of Game*—a famous fifteenth-century book on hunting, with beautiful illustrations.

For ' Town Life ' : Riley, *Memorials of London*—a huge collection of extracts from the City records, containing a mass of varied information ; the published *Records* of other towns, such as Norwich, Leicester, Northampton, and Reading ; Miss Dormer Harris, *Life in an Old English Town* ; Mrs. Green, *Town Life in the Fifteenth Century* ; Gomme, *The Making of London* ; Besant, *Medieval London* ; Furley, *Government of Winchester* ; Hughes and Lamborn, *Town Planning*.

For ' Home Life ' : Thomas Wright, *Domestic Manners and Sentiments in England* ; Hubert Hall, *Court Life under the Plantagenets* ; *The Babees Book* (Early English Text Soc.)—a fascinating collection of medieval books of etiquette, &c., with excellent notes by Dr. Furnivall.

For ' Religion ' : Gasquet, *Parish Life*, and *Monastic Life*—both read-able, but written with a strong Roman Catholic bias, which makes them often misleading ; Cutts, *Parish Priests and their People* ; Jessopp, *The Coming of the Friars* ; A. H. Thompson, *English Monasteries* ; the twelfth century *Chronicle of Jocelin of Brakelond*.

For ' Education ' : the works of A. F. Leach on Schools, and of Rait Rashdall, and Bass Mullinger on Universities.

For ' Arts and Science ' : mention may be made of the architectural works of Francis Bond, C. J. Cox, and Prof. Lethaby ; A. H. Thompson *The English Parish Church* and *Military Architecture* ; Parker and Turner *English Medieval Domestic Architecture* ; E. S. Prior, *English Medieval Art* the same writer's *Medieval Figure Sculpture*, Crossley's *English Church Monuments*, and the volume on *Westminster Abbey* published by the ' Royal Commission on National Monuments ' are three magnificent picture-books of English art.

For ' Literature ' : Pearsall Smith, *The English Language* ; Ker, *English Literature—Medieval* ; Jusserand, *Literary History of the English People* and such works as *The Cambridge History of English Literature*. For those who wish to consult originals for themselves the works of the ' Early English Text Society ' are a library in themselves, and prefaces and notes are a perfect mine of information.

For ' Law and Order ' : most of the works on this subject are intended for specialists—e.g. Pollock and Maitland, *History of English Law*. *The Court Baron* (Selden Soc.) contains a vivid picture of a manorial court in operation, and the published Records of various towns, already referred to, contain a good deal on the subject.

For ' Industry and Trade ' : Salzman, *Medieval English Industries* ; the works of Ashley, Cunningham, and Lipson on ' Economic History ' ; C. M Waters, *Economic History of England* ; Unwin, *Gilds and Companies of London*.

For ' War ' : J. Morris, *The Welsh Wars of Edward I* ; Oman, *History of the Art of Warfare* ; Demmin, *History of Arms and Armour* ; ffoulkes, *The Armourer and his Craft* ; Sir Guy Laking, *Arms and Armour*—five magnificent volumes. For ' Heraldry ' : the article on that subject in the *Encyclopaedia Britannica*, and the works of Sir William St. John Hope.

For ' Women ' : T. Wright, *Womankind in Western Europe* ; Miss Power, *English Nunneries*.

For ' Travel ' : Jusserand, *English Wayfaring Life in the Middle Ages* ; Hakluyt, *Voyages*, vol. I.

INDEX

PRINTED IN
GREAT BRITAIN
AT THE
UNIVERSITY PRESS
OXFORD
BY
JOHN JOHNSON
PRINTER
TO THE
UNIVERSITY